HUMAN RIGHTS IN RELIGIOUS TRADITIONS

HUMAN RIGHTS
IN RELIGIOUS TRADITIONS

Edited by Arlene Swidler

The Pilgrim Press
New York

Library of Congress Cataloging in Publication Data
Main entry under title:

Human rights in religious traditions.

  Bibliography: p. 111
  1. Civil rights—Religious aspects—Comparative studies—Addresses, essays, lectures.
  I. Swidler, Arlene.
BL65.C58H85   1982   291.1'77   82-15014
ISBN 0-8298-0633-4 (pbk.)

The Pilgrim Press, 132 West 31 Street, New York, New York 10001

CONTENTS

INTRODUCTION

The term "human rights" is comparatively new. Neither the term nor the concept is traditional in religious thought. Nevertheless, human rights represent what is probably the primary ethical concern in the world today. And, dealing as they do with our basic understanding of what it means to be human, what we are doing on this earth, and how we ought to relate to one another, human rights are at the center of religious thought and practice.

This collection of essays is an attempt at two kinds of collaboration. First, the *Journal of Ecumenical Studies* invited representatives of the world's major religions to lay out what they saw as the attitude of their own tradition toward human rights. These authors have approached their tasks with certain basic questions in mind, questions which the reader can expect to find tackled in at least some, and sometimes all, the essays:

- How might the term "human rights" be defined in each tradition?
- What specific areas would the concept embrace?
- Where does the theoretical basis for human rights lie—in scriptures, in philosophy, in tradition?
- How has thinking on human rights evolved?
- Which areas have been developed most successfully, and in which is further development still necessary?
- To what extent have human rights been upheld in societies dominated by these religions?
- And where, if at all, can we find a basis for an interfaith dialogue or consensus on human rights?

There are clear contrasts in the essays. Where J. Robert Nelson shows the strong biblical grounding for much of Protestantism's stance on human rights, John Langan stresses the philosophical basis in Roman Catholic thought. There are strong similarities as well. Stanley Harakas' emphasis on the relationship of rights to duties in Eastern Orthodox thought, for example, is echoed in Kana Mitra's essay, in which she explores human rights in Hinduism in terms of *dharma*.

Aspects of some of these theological essays may suggest new avenues for other traditions to investigate. Daniel Polish describes human-rights themes in the traditional celebrations of Judaism. Riffat Hassan points out in her essay on Islam how easily the ideals of human rights can be eroded. Kenneth Inada, writing from the Buddhist tradition, stresses the inseparability of the human-rights issues from the greater question of human nature.

The second type of collaboration will be seen in the essays which follow the theological presentations. For these, scholars from a variety of disciplines were invited to read the first essays and comment on them from their own perspectives. What, they were asked, do you as a specialist see in these essays that might not be apparent to the rest of us? And what do you as a specialist find lacking in these essays? The materials—it was assumed—on which the various religious traditions must theologize in this question of human rights will come to a large extent from other disciplines. Theology must then remain open to dialogue with and critique from these disciplines.

The results are as rich and varied as one could hope for. Besides bringing specialized facts and complex insights from their own work and research, these four specialists illuminate our whole general approach to the problems. Psychiatrist Perry Ottenberg warns of the difficulties religious people may find in overcoming defensiveness and confronting themselves with the appropriate questions on human rights. Hendrik B. Koning, an expert on technology, stresses the need for ongoing interdisciplinary dialogue. The essay by economist Noel J. J. Farley points out the problems arising when religious teaching on social issues is itself so diverse. Social historian Dennis J. Clark writes of the wide range of roles and tasks the theological community must assume if human rights are to be protected.

Two appendices conclude this collection. The first is the United Nations Universal Declaration of Human Rights, to which many of the writers here refer. The second consists of brief bibliographies for readers who wish to go more deeply into the whole human-rights issue.

The writers and I are pleased that The Pilgrim Press of New York has shown its concern for human rights by bringing out this collection of essays as *Human Rights in Religious Traditions*.

Arlene Swidler

Arlene Swidler (Roman Catholic) is Adjunct Professor of Religious Studies at Villanova University. She holds M.A.'s in English from the University of Wisconsin and in Theology from Villanova. A co-founder of the *Journal of Ecumenical Studies*, she has served as Managing Editor and Education Editor. Many of her numerous publications deal with the role of women in religion.

HUMAN RIGHTS IN RELIGIOUS TRADITIONS

1.

HUMAN RIGHTS IN CREATION AND REDEMPTION: A PROTESTANT VIEW

J. Robert Nelson

I. Protestantism's Varied History: A Brief, Personal Appraisal

Concern for the integrity, worth, and dignity of persons is the basic presupposition of human rights. At least three personal freedoms are requisite: freedom of conscience, freedom from unjust exploitation or oppression, and freedom to live a properly human life. Christian faith, as based upon biblical teaching and expressed in the experience of believers through the centuries, assuredly affirms these freedoms. Many theologians, scripture scholars, and Christian philosophers have cogently argued that "freedom" is a primary code word of the New Testament. In his person and his teaching, Jesus was the Liberator! This claim is not mere rhetoric.

Of the three main divisions of Christianity, Protestantism enjoys the best, but not an unsullied, reputation for securing, extending, and enhancing human freedoms. Indeed, there is a popular, well-preserved stereotype which portrays Protestant history as a series of successes in emancipating people for the enjoyment of greater freedom. The contrasting corollary to this image is that of Roman Catholicism as a perennial Inquisition. Catholic history is depicted as unrelieved servitude in subjection to hierarchical authority, freedom of conscience being stifled by the imposition of unreasonable, outrageously dogmatic restraints upon children, women, and men. Eastern Orthodoxy, especially the notorious early Byzantine and the Russian, has a similar reputation. Such are the views, as widely held as they are uncritical and uninformed, of many Protestants.

There is truth in both the positive picture of Protestantism and the negative judgments on Orthodoxy and Catholicism. However, inversely considered, history shows in varying measures the grave faults of Protestantism in this regard and the virtues of the other two. Ambiguity taints the entire history of Christianity insofar as human rights are concerned. Martin Luther began the Reformation by proclaiming a basic paradox. The freedom of the Christian is at the same time a bondage. The freest person is, in Christ, the servant of all. But Protestants have often been inclined to exalt two kinds of bondage: that to the Christ perceived in one's neighbor, and that demanded by ecclesiastical and civil powers.

J. Robert Nelson (United Methodist) is Professor of Systematic Theology at the Boston University School of Theology. An ordained minister, he received his D. Theol. from the University of Zurich. He has served as Secretary of the Commission on Faith and Order of the World Council of Churches and as a member of the United States Commission for UNESCO. His most recent book is *Science and Our Troubled Conscience*. He has been an Associate Editor of the *Journal of Ecumenical Studies* since 1974.

Neither the Lutherans nor the Calvinists but the "left wing" Christians of the Reformation of the sixteenth century were the direct predecessors of the most energetic movements for freedom from oppression by princely and prelatic power. From them came such effective disturbers of entrenched conservatism as the Baptists, Mennonites, and Quakers. Luther's conception of freedom for all people in the civil sphere hardly found exemplary expression in Germany or the Scandinavian countries, where the Lutheran churches enjoyed a status both favored and established. Present-day Lutheranism to a considerable extent has been liberated and has become a liberating faith. Calvinism has fared rather better, despite a checkered history, as stimulus and tutor to human rights. Calvinism did spawn some excesses of theocratic suppression of liberties in Geneva and Massachusetts, while paradoxically giving rise to the political movement of covenanted, responsible democracy. (It is not coincidental that the constitutional document of Woodrow Wilson's League of Nations was called the Covenant, and the covenant concept persists in the United Nations' program to further human rights.)

Between ideal concepts of human rights, dignity, and happiness and their general realization in society there is always a disappointing hiatus. Ruthless monarchy or totalitarianism has shown a much higher capacity to be incorporated into political structures and social relations than have democratic ideals of liberty. The same disjunction between ideal and reality applies to societies in which various forms of Protestantism have been determinative. Does this familiar condition, then, discredit and disqualify the claim that Protestant Christianity merits much—but by no means all—credit for the upsurge of popular affirmations of rights? No. But honesty requires a mental check on one's enthusiasm for extolling Protestantism as a whole for its contribution. Protestant churches and theologies are too diverse to be treated as a unity. The historical record is too ambiguous to merit unequivocal praise. Yet, the positive influences have been, and remain, real.

II. The Individual or the Community, or Both?

Individualism, according to a popular notion, is the hallmark of Protestantism. Such slogans as "the private interpretation of the Bible" or "a man and his God" reinforce this idea. The passing ideal of "the rugged individualist" has often been equated with the true Protestant. Having this understanding, one who reads the 1948 Universal Declaration of Human Rights[1] might readily assume that it is a very Protestant document. Nearly all the thirty specific articles employ the singular subject and verb. "Everyone" has rights. "No one" shall be deprived of these rights. In the case of parents and family in Article 16, of

---

[1]See pp. 105-109, below.

course, the plural has to be used. Otherwise, the Declaration appears to be entirely individualistic.

"And why not?" asks a Protestant Christian. "Isn't that what our faith is about?" Yes and no; the answer must be equivocal. In most of its theological types and ecclesial shapes, Protestantism enhances the eminence of the individual person. Private judgment in matters of faith is equated with freedom of conscience. Personal responsibility in morals and ethics may not be evaded. Personal prayer and worship may not be accomplished by a priest on the individual's behalf. Christian faith, then, is the concern of the individual, but it is never individualistic.

It is manifestly the case that Protestant belief generally supports the value and integrity of each human being. There is no alternative in belief and theory to holding each person to be of "infinite value," as liberal Protestants usually say. Why? Because God created each one; God loves each one; and Jesus Christ died for the sins of each one that each might be saved. Inasmuch as you did an act of mercy for one of the least of these persons, you did it for Jesus Christ. One of the least! No one is left out. The Creator who marks the fall to earth of each perishing sparrow surely holds dearer by far each human person. These and similar biblical insights and affirmations are fundamental to the religious and moral perspective held by Protestants.

The claim of one person, however, to require satisfaction of a given human right cannot in all cases be held to be absolute. The right of one member of the community must not be used to override the well-being of the whole, any more than the whole community may annul the right of any one member. The individual always exists in community, and it is within this community that the truly personal character of the individual's life is realized. For many Protestants, with all their high regard for the individual's rights and value, it is the intimacy and solidarity of members of the community which are the distinctive signs of their concept of the church.

The teaching of the apostle Paul on this question is authoritative in two ways: if one member suffers or is honored, all in the community likewise suffer or enjoy honor; but, whatever their individually received gifts may be, all must strive to build up the church in love (1 Cor. 12:26; 14:12). So the understanding of the church as the Body of Christ is as much a Protestant as it is an Orthodox or Catholic one, however differently interpreted. Paul gave an exemplary instance of the application of human rights within a communal context when he instructed the Corinthian Christians about their dispute over eating sacrificed meat. In the pagan custom of the Roman Empire the meat from animals offered to idols was later sold in the market and served at table. Some very sensitive Christians believed and feared that it would amount to the terrible sin of idolatry to eat such meat. Paul disagreed. In modern idiom he would have said, "I have a perfect right to eat that meat. There is no divine law against doing so." For the sake of his own sense of dignity and for the apostolic authority of his office he could have insisted on this permissive belief. He chose not to insist.

Rather than give offense to another member of the Christian community and thus bring deplorable dissension into the church, Paul suspended his right to eat that meat. The right of the individual was here subordinated to the welfare of the community, but it was a freely chosen abstinence in which his right was weighed against a more important responsibility (1 Cor. 8).

The polities of Protestant churches both reflect and influence the distinction between the priority of the individual and of the community with respect to rights. Protestant communions are organized, administered, and maintained by quite diverse canons or polities, but all rest upon one of two general concepts of the church's nature. The first gives priority to the whole organically structured communion or denomination because it believes the church to be the given social entity—the Body of Christ or Household of God—into which persons are brought. By baptism, usually as an infant, and subsequent confirmation, one is made a church member. The identity of individual members is neither dissolved nor lost in the organic community, however. Like "living stones" they become parts of the corporate "temple" (1 Pet. 2:5), but not as inert, identical bricks in the church's fabric. As in all serious versions of ecclesiology, the member's personal standing is presumed to be enhanced by belonging to this earthly historical form of Christ's existence, the Body. Communions so characterized usually have an episcopal or a presbyterian order.

The second concept of the church is that of the free, voluntary association of believers. Here, Christian individuals come together and are gathered in the fellowship of faith, worship, communal life, and mission. As with the organic concept, personal individuality is enhanced by this life in community, but the main difference lies in the sense of priority. "Do not the believers precede the organization of the church?" they ask. The church is not simply *there*, awaiting the initiation and entrance of the member. In this "gathered church" concept the individual (at least in theological thought) precedes, and the polity is usually congregational. During four centuries it has been the type of ecclesiological concept which has contributed to the most overt and persistent championing of human rights. Such churches are often, but unclearly, called "free churches." This is unclear because in the United States they are not "free" as opposed to "established," but "free" in their congregational voluntarism. Where such Protestant communities have thrived in Western Europe, Great Britain, and North America, the general popular attitude favors emphasis upon the rights of individual persons over against the rights of society.

It may be reasonably argued, and should be noted, that other influences—apart from religion in general or Protestantism in particular—have also accounted for the primacy of the individual's rights in these countries. Philosophical ideas about individual liberty have emanated from the Renaissance in Europe, the Enlightenment in Britain and America, the Rationalism of Revolutionary France, and Democratic Humanism since the nineteenth century. While these philosophies have been in some serious ways inimical to Christian faith and the churches, they have, nevertheless, been congenial to the Protestant theology which upholds the right and autonomy of each person as prior to society's right. Thus it is easy to see why secular movements for civil rights and justice have found more willing cooperation by certain Protestants than by others, or by the Orthodox and Roman Catholics.

III. The Impact of Social, Economic, Cultural, and Political Factors

It is interesting to note how the prevailing social and political character of a given country can affect the meaning which Protestants attach to human rights. The affecting power of Marxism is conspicuous, for example, in the socialist countries of Europe. As will be discussed below, an important ecumenical consultation was held in 1974 at St. Pölten, Austria, under auspices of the Commission of the Churches on International Affairs (CCIA) of the World Council of Churches. The Roman Catholic Church does not belong to the Council, however friendly may be its relations to it, so the consultation was composed almost wholly of Protestant and Orthodox participants. A working group of Christians in the predominantly Protestant German Democratic Republic submitted a paper on human rights. These persons were not at all disposed to regard the rights of individuals as prior to those of society. On grounds of biblical teaching, they contended that "the inviolability of life, dignity and property are not a constitutive element of the human being," since these rights belong to God.[2] They argued, moreover, that civil rights such as free opinion and speech subvert "the political and moral unity of the people [which] are fundamental requirements of the new society." When individual rights are allowed to cause "the disintegration of society into a multiplicity of conflicting groups," they serve only to reinforce "capitalist structures which depend on the competitive struggle and conflict among human beings."[3]

The difference between the two perspectives on the relation of the individual to the whole are sharply delineated here. To the democratic Protestant-minded person of a capitalist country, the defense and preservation of individual rights are indispensable to the maintenance of a free society. Such rights always imply their responsible exercise, of course, in any and all contexts. Where rights are protected and used responsibly, the conditions for a tolerably good democracy are enhanced. By contrast, the German Protestants who support state-controlled socialism insist that the needs for building a just and equitable society determine the kinds of rights that people may enjoy at any time.

Which of these contrasting positions is the authentically Protestant one? The presence of the contrast at least illustrates the diversity of understanding of human rights among Protestants as well as the power of ideological influences to

[2]"The Meaning of Human Rights and the Problems They Pose," *The Ecumenical Review* 27 (April, 1975): 143.
[3]Ibid., p. 140.

affect the understanding. The problem is further complicated by the recent upheaval in Poland caused by the Solidarity movement. Rights to free speech, assembly, press, labor organizations, and political participation were being demanded and secured by Roman Catholics in a socialist state! The traditional stereotypes are really breaking down.

It is no longer justifiable to allow the distorted characterizations of the three main Christian types. The many Eastern Orthodox Christians are not committed to support the caesaro-papism as it once prevailed under the emperor or czar. Roman Catholics do not allow the obsequious attitude which prevails in the Vatican curia to dampen their zeal for human rights in various countries where they are strong—especially in view of the great encyclicals of recent popes which have sounded the clarion call for universal respect of human dignity, rights, and development. And Protestants as a whole are not always the freedom-loving contenders for a genuinely democratic society, although many of them continue to be such.

The reason for the breaking down of these traditional images and the consequent blurring of distinctions among Christian churches and among theologies of human freedom is simply the powerful effect of the varying social and political theories which are implemented in the economic systems and structures of government. Protestants are numerous and strong in Finland, as well as in Switzerland, South Africa, Tanzania, and the German Democratic Republic. How does that fact signify what their understandings of human rights may be? Only by examining the respective economies, political institutions, and regnant social mores in these countries can a fair reading be made of their religiously conditioned views of human rights.

Another necessity for accurate understanding is the discerning of great differences between two kinds of human rights. One may be called "rights to be secured"; the other, "rights to be provided for and satisfied." The important distinction was boldly drawn by the General Assembly of the United Nations in 1966, when it adopted the two covenants: the International Covenant of Civil and Political Rights and that of Economic, Social and Cultural Rights. These covenants (again using the Calvinistic nomenclature) are still in the process of being ratified by member states.[4]

A reading of the Universal Declaration of 1948 reveals both categories. However, the civil and political rights are manifestly dominant in twenty-three of the thirty articles. These twenty-three express the basic freedoms and expectations of all persons which, according to the Declaration, must be secured by every national government for its citizens. In the philosophy of the Declaration, these rights are inherent in human life as such, although history quickly teaches us that only in modern times have they been widely so recognized. These are the individual's claims upon society and civil government for protecting and guaran-

---

[4]Sean McBride, "The Universal Declaration—Thirty Years After," in Alan D. Falconer, ed., *Understanding Human Rights* (Dublin: Irish School of Ecumenics, 1980), pp. 10-13.

teeing free exercise of the rights of speech, press, assembly, religion, mobility, privacy, legal defense, and marriage and family life. They are the civil and political rights which are protected, at least in word, by many national constitutions. For the most part they articulate the general Protestant concern for individual freedom and civic responsibility within a parliamentary, democratic society. In particular, Article 18 declares the religious right to a free conscience, belief, worship, teaching, and voluntary change of faith. (According to the account of the late Dr. Elfan Rees of the World Council of Churches' CCIA, this article was included in the Declaration only because of the persistent and diplomatic pressures of his ecumenical group in Paris. The Roman Catholic Church had not yet made its remarkable *volte face* on the subject of religious liberty, even though the Papal Nuncio, Cardinal Angelo Roncalli, used his personal influence in Paris to impress upon the United Nations authorities his convictions about human rights—which later appeared in his great encyclical when he became Pope John XXIII.)

The other seven articles define rights which cannot simply be secured by constitutions, legislation, or governmental policies and programs. They depend entirely upon the economic resources of a nation, whether indigenous or received as foreign aid.

Ideally considered, every person should have title to property, choice of gainful employment, holidays with pay, adequate food and shelter, education, health care, and old-age security. If these are called rights, however, they cannot be satisfied sufficiently by an impoverished nation; are they then rights or only human desiderata?[5] Certain nations are so utterly poor that they can hardly begin to provide for all the social, economic, and cultural rights so defined. Others, of whatever degree of wealth, can satisfy the claims only by a relative equalizing of resources so as to achieve a leveling of expenditure for the good things required and desired by all. Certainly this kind of general sharing is in accord with the Christian belief about mutual support in a motivating attitude of love. It also conforms to the recently emphasized biblical theme that "God is on the side of the poor."[6]

The fact that constitutions and laws in some nations cannot satisfy social, economic, and cultural rights does not reduce or eliminate them as being very important for human living. It only indicates that these claims are inseparable from the civil and political ones. The rights listed under the two United Nations covenants are of different kinds, but they are interrelated at many points.

The notion that a person can be destitute and yet be civilly and politically free is a romantic myth. Monks of various religions may choose a life of holy

---

[5]Gustaf Wingren criticized the tendency to inflate the concept of rights until a totally welfare-state economy is presupposed, in "Human Rights: A Theological Analysis," *The Ecumenical Review* 27 (April, 1975): 126.

[6]See José Miguez-Bonino, "Religious Commitment and Human Rights," in Falconer, *Understanding Human Rights*, pp. 28-29; and Julio de Santa Ana, *Good News to the Poor* (Geneva: World Council of Churches, 1977).

poverty—owning nothing and begging for food—but, for those who abhor poverty, there is no holiness in it: only misery and revolting degradation. Moreover, they suffer infringement of the rights of both covenants because they must live in poverty. Millions of black persons, for example, are effectually, if not always legally, deprived of civil, political, and other rights, because their poverty makes them powerless. They are poor and powerless because they are black, and, for this reason, they are victims of white racism. Racism in many instances causes widespread deprivation of rights. Racism is totally contradictory and repugnant to the Christian faith. White racism is the most dangerous of all kinds of ethnocentrism, because the largest measure of economic and military power belongs to the world's white minority. It is the blunt and brutal reality of this aspect of human rights which today causes greatest concern to the members of Protestant churches.

The World Council of Churches is the most widely representative forum of Protestant Christians, who fortunately meet always with many Orthodox and some Roman Catholics. Therefore, the St. Pölten consultation of 1974 and its sequel of discussions in the Fifth Assembly of the Council at Nairobi, Kenya, in 1975, have provided significant statements on human rights.

Seeking to formulate an ecumenical agreement on priorities in basic human rights, the St. Pölten delegates concurred on six,[7] which became the framework for deliberation at Nairobi.[8] They may be paraphrased as follows:

a. the primary right to life, including both the preservation and quality of life;

b. the right to enjoy cultural identity and self-determination for both individuals and peoples and nations;

c. the right to participate in a democratic process of decision-making on matters affecting one's life;

d. the right to hold one's own opinion and to dissent from others;

e. the right to personal dignity and to expect fair treatment before the law by political powers; and

f. the right to choose freely one's faith and religion, and to practice and exercise that religion.

These six are mainly of a civil and political nature, but the first is an open door to a large assortment of social, economic, and cultural rights. However, as noted, unless these latter rights can also be provided for in large measure, the former can have little meaning for people.

In the extensive report on human rights adopted by the Nairobi Assembly, the emphasis fell upon the urgent need to implement practical measures to

---

[7]*Human Rights and Christian Responsibility*. Report of the Consultation, St. Pölten, Austria, 21-26 October 1974 (Geneva: World Council of Churches, 1975).

[8]David M. Paton, ed., *Breaking Barriers, Nairobi 1975* (Grand Rapids, MI: Wm. B. Eerdmans, 1976), pp. 103-106.

protect, secure, and satisfy many of the rights on which there is virtually universal agreement. No more formal declarations need to be drafted for the present. The United Nations' Declaration and the two covenants provide all the agenda which the peoples of the world can handle for a century to come. Yet, it is most encouraging that the U.N. General Assembly in December, 1981, after twenty years of deliberation and drafting, approved the "Declaration on the Elimination of All Forms of Intolerance and of Discrimination Based on Religion or Belief."

Since it has been agreed that the six rights are of highest priority, Christians acting together in their churches and nations and in ecumenical cooperation need to attack the root causes, not the symptoms, of the violation of rights. Those causes which "create the conditions under which human rights are denied [are] economic exploitation, political manipulation, military power, class domination, psychological conditioning."[9] Religious thought and social philosophies have provided the concepts and ideas upon which declarations of human rights can be drafted, but the lists are only words until people and nations begin to act seriously to make them work for human enjoyment. It is not of the nature of Protestant belief to think that the churches as such can remake or reform whole societies and nations according to the canons of Christian morality. Since the theocratic notion which Calvin cherished is no longer held, Christianity today differs markedly from Islam in this regard. Nevertheless, the power of Christian churches in many lands, or the potential power, is such as to challenge the churches to exercise it more vigorously and courageously for the sake of human rights than has recently been the case.

IV. Explorations for a Theological Rationale

Thomas Jefferson regarded "inalienable" rights as "self-evident" endowments by the Creator. A decade after Jefferson's quill had written these famous words, the French revolutionary theorists attributed les droites de l'homme et du citoyen to nature and reason. Neither of these concepts of rights was the product of explicit religious thought. It is more likely that Jefferson's deism and the French rationalism were derived from a mélange of Greek philosophy, Jewish and Christian biblical teachings, Renaissance humanism, and John Locke.[10] When the United Nations delegates arrived at agreement on so many specific rights, they represented a broader range of philosophical traditions and ideologies than did eighteenth-century thinking. Oriental ideas, as well as Marxism-Leninism, were added to the mixture. Yet, remarkably, they all did concur! What could be a clearer evidence for the universality of the Declaration?

Many Christian churches also accepted the human rights as being consistent

---

[9]Ibid., p. 102.
[10]Miguez-Bonino, "Religious Commitment," p. 24.

10

with their faith—not only consistent, but even expressive of their faith. It would have seemed, therefore, that all these rights were truly self-evident, whatever their natural or supernatural source. So why should Christians try to build a theological foundation under a structure which already seems to be firmly founded? Could not the churches simply "baptize" the human rights and so adopt them as their own? Church bodies and individual Christians have done just that. Then, in retrospect, they have sought to show that the United Nations managed to make explicit many of the admonitions and promises which are already implicit in the Bible. Some with special enthusiasm have been further inclined to affirm human rights as a kind of international civil religion which comprehends "the highest truths" of all religions and humane ideologies.

Inspiring and useful as is this quasi-religious belief for promoting what the United Nations—in pre-feminist years—styled a "spirit of brotherhood" among all human beings (Article 1), it may seem scandalous that a respected Anglican theologian, David Jenkins, wrote: "I do not believe that the notion of human rights is at all biblical."[11] But this startling remark deserves a hearing and testing. Biblical passages can indeed be selected to undergird the affirmation of certain rights, as we have seen above. But what can be said about so "self-evident" a prohibition as Article 4 against slavery, when the New Testament admonishes slaves to "be submissive to your masters" (1 Pet. 2:18)? Nor can the right to daily food (Article 25) be reconciled with Paul's strong dictum, "If anyone will not work, let him not eat" (2 Thess. 3:10). And one can hardly imagine an exemplary Christian who lives in strict conformity to Jesus' Sermon on the Mount demanding rights to anything, since selflessness and submission are Jesus' rule for life in the Reign of God. Examples can be multiplied to demonstrate that the only self-evident right in the Bible is the sovereign right of God over creation and creatures.

The World Council of Churches was inaugurated in the same year that the Declaration was adopted, 1948. Ever since, human rights have been a constant concern of the Council. Practical acceptance of the rights and progress to implement them have prevailed over theological testing, however. The St. Pölten consultation recognized this deficiency. Why a deficiency? Because Christians have a well-formulated theological rationale for everything they do? No, but this is an intellectualistic inclination on the part of professional theologians.

What we find in the Bible is nothing like a catalog of rights. Even when the counterpart of rights is stressed, namely, responsible obedience to God and love of neighbor, the idea of naturally endowed rights is strange to the biblical writings. What the Bible and the Christian faith in fidelity to it do extol are the distinct, irreplaceable value of human beings and the possibility that each person may enjoy the fulfillment of life on earth. In the Gospel of John, Jesus says most significantly, "I came that they might have life, and have it abundantly"

[11]David Jenkins, "Human Rights in Christian Perspective," *Study Encounter*, vol. 10, no. 2 (1974), p. 2.

(Jn. 10:10). This is a key concept in the Christian appraisal of human life, its value, and its possibilities. Authentic, fully realized, eternal life is the offer of God in Jesus Christ to all who will accept it. As the St. Pölten report stated:

> It is our conviction that the emphasis of the Gospel is upon the value of all human beings in the sight of God, on the atoning and redeeming work of Christ that has given to man his true dignity, on love as the motive for action, and on love for one's neighbor as the practical expression of an active faith in Christ.[12]

Two worldwide organizations of Protestant churches have not been satisfied with so general a theological basis for human rights and have sought their own. They are the bodies which continue the two main streams of the sixteenth-century Reformation: the Lutheran World Federation and the World Alliance of Reformed Churches. Both are noted for their strong bent toward finding theological terms on which their various churches can agree. The clarifications found by these two bodies may be summarized very briefly here.

The Lutherans adopted a three-fold pattern into which all rights may fit, the key words being freedom, equality, and participation.[13] None of these categories is proposed as a simple, unambiguous basis of appeal for rights. Howsoever a person is justified or made right with God by the confession of faith in the righteous God made known in Jesus Christ, that person remains at the same time sinful. (*Simul justus et peccator* is the Lutheran formula.) Lutherans pose no perfectionist ideals of freedom, equality, and participation, as the nearly similar words of the French Revolution convey. The freest person is the one in bondage of responsible love to others; the equality of persons inheres in their standing before God, who made them all in the divine image; and participation in the upbuilding of a society in which children, women, and men enjoy increasingly the various rights is a matter of committing oneself unreservedly to the mutuality of a community. So Lutherans do not simply "baptize" the United Nations Declaration, but they see in its rights the secular analogies to the essential terms of the Gospel by which all persons should be able to live.

The Reformed, or Calvinist, theologians perceived a different triad of principles for grounding human rights. They followed the lead of Tübingen theologian Jürgen Moltmann, to whom leadership in their quest entrusted. Moltmann set human rights in the threefold formula: liberation by Jesus Christ, creation in the image of God, and hope in the coming Reign of God.[14] These are

---

[12]See note 7, above.

[13]J. Lissner, ed., *Theological Perspectives on Human Rights* (Geneva: Lutheran World Federation, 1977). This study is ably discussed in relation to Roman Catholic and Reformed Protestant thinking by Agnes Cunningham, Donald Miller, and James Will in "Toward an Ecumenical Theology for Human Rights," photocopied for the National Council of Churches, New York, in 1980.

[14]Jan Milic Lochman, "Um eine christliche Perspektive für die Menschenrechte," *Reformatio* 25 (July-August, 1976): 418; and Jürgen Moltmann, "Christian Faith and Human

dynamic, not static, concepts. As translated into the language of rights, they speak of the activity of God in human history, recreating in Christ the persons who were first created in the divine image, and providing them hope, despite privation and suffering, for liberation of life in society to its fulfillment in God's purpose. Like the Lutherans, the Reformed subsume rights—and all human matters—under the sovereignty of God, who creates and redeems. Human rights are not, therefore, given in the laws of creation, in natural law. As noted above, in the biblical view only God has rights over all creatures, with whom, by God's grace, an enduring covenant has been made. Thus, the breakdown of human rights into many specific ones is our way of analyzing the ways by which our human acts and relations may fulfill our side of the covenant.

In these Protestant views, the universality of God's care for all persons is believed to be offered through the particularity of Jesus Christ, not as a demand but as a gift. Rights which are defined according to other religious and philosophical premises are honored, to be sure. But they mean for Christians more than the conditions for a relatively good and happy life. In short, human rights belong to our redemption, not just to our creation.

Rights," in Falconer, *Understanding Human Rights*, pp. 182-195. See A. O. Miller, ed., *A Christian Declaration of Human Rights* (Grand Rapids, MI: Wm. B. Eerdmans, 1977), for related material.

2.

HUMAN RIGHTS:
AN EASTERN ORTHODOX PERSPECTIVE

Stanley S. Harakas

I. Introduction

Eastern Orthodox Christianity is distinguished from Roman Catholicism and Protestantism by its self-understanding as continuing in unbroken continuity the undivided unity of the early church in an essentially unchanged form with regard to doctrine, worship, ethical teaching, and church organization. Based on the Holy Scriptures and the commonly inherited Holy Tradition of the Apostolic Church, Eastern Orthodoxy believes itself to be one with and the same as the early undivided Christian church. For its positions on contemporary moral and social issues, the Eastern Orthodox Church draws on the whole living experience of the early church, including the Old and New Testaments, the writings of the Church Fathers, the decisions and canons of the Ecumenical Councils, and the liturgical tradition, as well as the acts and ethos of the church throughout the centuries. These sources form the bases of Orthodox Christian theological thought and ethical teaching.

It is on this long-standing and rich tradition that an Orthodox position on the issue of human rights has been developed. In this discussion of human rights from an Eastern Orthodox Christian perspective I will draw on this 2,000-year tradition of ecclesial history to define human rights, to examine the extent of human rights, to explicate some of the foundations of human rights, to note developments in the applications of human-rights principles, to examine the actual realization of human rights among the Eastern Orthodox, and, finally, to look at an Orthodox contribution to consensus on human rights.

II. The Meaning of Human Rights

The traditional mode of thinking in Orthodoxy recognizes that few, if any, of the things which are of ultimate concern for human beings are readily defined. For example, when speaking of God, Orthodoxy prefers to speak apophatically (negatively), recognizing that no human concepts can capture the essence of God. Even when Orthodox Christians speak kataphatically (positively) about God, these statements will tend to affirm truths about God which are paradoxical, that is, which are affirmed to be true and yet, according to mere human

Stanley S. Harakas (Greek Orthodox) is a Professor of Christian Ethics at Holy Cross School of Theology, Brookline, MA, where he was previously Dean. He holds a Th.D. from Boston University. Father Harakas' most recent book is *For the Health of Body and Soul: An Introduction to Orthodox Bioethics*.

14

reason, stand in some sort of contradiction to each other. This is true because of the ultimate transcendence of God to the created world.

In similar, though much less intense, fashion are definitions about moral issues addressed. No definition is ever fully adequate. All definitions exaggerate some aspects while minimizing other aspects of a moral issue. Such is the case with "human rights."

The first thing which needs to be noted is that human rights, in and of themselves, are not directly addressed in the modern fashion by the early Christian tradition. This is because the tradition tends to focus more on duties and responsibilities than on rights, more on the call to achieve our human potential by overcoming sin and distortion in life through a synergy of Divine Grace and the exercise of spiritual self-discipline than by claiming it as a right to be granted by others. The tradition emphasizes the idea that love more often than not requires sacrifice of one's "rights" than the insistence upon them, and forgiveness of their violation by others than insistence upon their fulfillment. The Eastern Orthodox Christian approach to life as a whole tends not to be cast in a legalistic *quid quo pro* framework but, rather, in the imitation of God as giving, grace-filled, compassionate, forgiving, looking toward a communion of human beings which reflects the loving communion of Father, Son, and Holy Spirit—the Holy Trinity.

However, on a much less prominent, though not insignificant, level there has been a concern with rights, especially the violated rights of others such as the weak, the poor, the abused, and the downtrodden. This concern with defending and justifying the rights of the weak, poor, and oppressed is based on the common, God-given humanity that all share, as will be seen below. As a result, when called to define rights, Orthodox Christian ethicists tend to define human rights not in themselves, but as the reciprocal side of duties or moral responsibilities. Thus, one Orthodox ethicist has written:

> The meaning of duty is inseparably bound up with the idea of right. Wherever there is a duty, there also exists a reciprocal right. . . . Accordingly, "right" is the legal or ethical demand of the person who fulfills his duties towards others that others reciprocally fulfill their duties toward him.[1]

But rights may also be seen as claims which one makes upon others as one's due, as something arising from one's very being. Another Orthodox author more broadly referred to "that which belongs to each person, that is, whatever is owed to and appropriate to each . . . , that is, whether one has the authority to do something or to demand something and receive from others that which is due one."[2]

---

[1]Panagiotes Demetropoulos, *Orthodoxos Christianike Ethike* (privately published, Athens, 1970), p. 112.
[2]Vasileios Antoniades, *Encheiridion Kata Christon Ethikes* (Constantinople: Fazilet Press, 1927), vol. 1, p. 147.

The first definition, based on reciprocity of duties and rights, derives its strength from the idea that all persons have moral demands placed on them; hence, their duties are the rights (just claims) of others upon their behavior. It also serves to explain why the rights of some persons, such as criminals, may be temporarily suspended as restraint or punishment when these persons fail to fulfill their duties toward others. This definition emphasizes the corporate and organic character of the exercise of rights and duties. The second definition focuses rather on the irreducible character of the human agent who is the bearer of rights and duties. At its simplest, one has rights and duties not because one does or does not do certain things, but because of who or what one is. "Being" is emphasized here. Rights are due a person simply and uniquely because he or she is a human being. This is easy to claim but much harder to support, especially from a secular perspective, and even more difficult to delineate.

III. Breadth, Depth, and Limits

What specific areas does the concept of rights embrace? There is a sense in which our rights are identified with every aspect of our humanness. In a passage in which the fourth-century Father, St. John Chrysostom, was arguing against returning evil treatment to those who do evil to us, because such action in fact destroys our own dignity, he pointed to the fact of his listeners' "*dikaiomata*," that is, "rights or claims" which they share with the person who would do them harm. Mentioning some of these, he called them "innumerable, . . . ten thousand other things," contrasting them with "innumerable evils."[3] If it is true that rights are the reverse coin of our moral duties and appropriate behavior on the one hand, and our "due" as human beings on the other, then both the moral complexity of life in the first case and the richness of our human capabilities in the second would tend to argue for innumerable rights. Our claims would then tend to multiply beyond what are normally designated as rights to embrace "ten thousand other things," such as when students of a certain state university in the U.S.A. recently protested a ban on coed campus toilets as a violation of their "human rights."[4]

It may be that human rights and human wants are thus confused. It is clear that there are limits to rights. The first limit which negates the trivialization of the reality of human rights is that which comes from the rights of others in community. No one lives alone as a human being; no person becomes human or exercises his or her humanity in isolation. The rights of others are limits to the exercise of my own rights. Further, rights are restricted to the sphere of morally acceptable behavior. Thus, the right to own property may not be exercised to

---

[3]*Hebrews*, xxv, 6.
[4]"Sit-in to protest ban on coed toilets," *The Daily Transcript* (Dedham, MA), October 14, 1981, p. 1.

the point where the right to life and existence is denied to others, nor can the right to liberty be the justification for any or every kind of immorality. One may be free and have the right to exercise that freedom, but that does not grant the right to steal, rape, or kill.

Another limitation, especially for those who seek to grow in the godlike expression of love, is the realization that concern for others may frequently call for a person not to claim or exercise rights which otherwise could be claimed for one's self. Thus St. Paul recognized that he could properly seek to be supported by the Christian communities to which he preached the gospel and to have a spouse, but, for the sake of that very gospel and its spread, he preferred not to do so and to earn his bread with his own hands.

> Do we not have the right to our food and drink? Do we not have the right to be accompanied by a wife as the other Apostles and the brothers of the Lord and Cephas? Or is it only Barnabas and I who have no right to refrain from working for a living? Who serves as a soldier at his own expense? Who plants a vineyard without eating any of its fruit? Who tends a flock without getting some of the milk? . . . If we have sown spiritual good among you, is it too much if we reap your material benefits? If others share this rightful claim upon you, do we not still more? Nevertheless, we have not made use of this right, but we endure anything rather than put an obstacle in the way of the gospel of Christ.[5]

In this passage, St. Paul clearly recognized not only the right to be supported by the churches he served but also the propriety of the claim that the right be recognized. Clearly others (the apostles, the brothers of the Lord, and even Peter) have exercised these rights. Thus, under normal circumstances, we will also have the duty to claim rights for ourselves. In the words of an authority in Greek Orthodox ethics:

> From the close relationship of duties to rights, it is clear that just as every human being is obligated to fulfill the requirements of duty, so, in the same manner, each ought to defend those rights which are based on those very same duties. Of course, there are those occasions according to which one may sacrifice one's own rights and forgive those who commit injustice against one for the sake of the greater good. But that in principle one ought to deny one's own rights as opposed in themselves to the meaning of love, this is based on a clearly erroneous understanding of love.[6]

It has been pointed out frequently that both Jesus Christ and the Apostle Paul at particular moments made claim for their own rights.[7] Note has been

---

[5]1 Cor. 9:4-7, 11-12. See also the balance of chap. 9.
[6]Chrestos Androutsos, *Systema Ethikes*, 2nd ed. (Thessalonica: Bas. Regopoulos Publishing House, 1964), p. 138.
[7]Jn. 18:23; Acts 16:37, 22:25.

made as well of the early church's claim of the right to religious freedom.[8] Yet the church's accent has been not on the claim of one's own rights or even the rights of the church itself, but rather on the concern for the violation of the rights of others—in particular, the weak and the poor and the defenseless. It is here that "rights" are most clearly identified. They are basic claims which all persons need to exist as human beings. They are the rights to life and health and to civil and religious freedom, the right to exercise an occupation to earn one's living, the right to ownership of basic necessities, the right to cultural and/or national identity, the right to marry and propagate progeny, the right to equal and fair treatment before the law, etc. Thus we have a record of early Christian concern with the rights of those who were oppressed and unable to defend their own rights. The early church was strongly opposed to abortion, as an example of the defense of the right to life. It was also opposed to the old Roman practice of the exposure of unwanted children. Such children either died or were "rescued" by persons who more often than not maimed them and used them either for begging or for purposes of prostitution.[9]

St. John Chrysostom, St. Basil, and other Church Fathers echoed the concern for the rights of the poor in contradistinction to their exploitation by the rich, without denying the right of others to earn wealth. Rather, they insisted that the best use and conservation of wealth was to share it with those who have a right to it, since in the beginning all shared the wealth of the world in common.[10] Human rights were also defended in the patristic condemnation of the institution of slavery in principle,[11] and through the church's influence on civil

---

[8]Thus, Athenagoras, an early (177 A.D.) apologist, wrote "A Plea for the Christians" to the then-reigning Roman emperors:

> . . . with admiration of your mildness and gentleness, and your peaceful and benevolent disposition toward every man, individuals live in the possession of equal rights. . . . But for us who are called Christians you have not in like manner cared; but although we commit no wrong . . . you allow us to be harassed, plundered and persecuted, the multitude making war upon us for our name alone. . . . What therefore is conceded as the common right of all, we claim for ourselves; that we shall not be hated and punished because we are called Christians . . . but be tried on any charges which may be brought against us, and either be released on our disproving them or punished if convicted of crime—not for the name . . . but for the wrong which has been done. . . . Let this equal justice be done to us.

Selected from chaps. 1 and 2 (*The Ante-Nicene Fathers* [Grand Rapids, MI: William B. Eerdmans Publishing Co., 1956], vol. 2, pp. 129-130).

[9]See C. J. Cadoux, *The Early Church and the World* (Edinburgh: T. & T. Clark, 1925); and Panagiotes Demetropoulos, *E Pistis tis Archaias Ekklesias os Kanon Zoes kai O Kosmos* (privately published, Athens, 1959).

[10]George Wolfgang Forell, *History of Christian Ethics* (Minneapolis: Augsburg, 1979), vol. 1, especially chaps. 6-8. Also see Panagiotis Chrestou, *E Koinoniologia to Megalou Basilliou* (privately published, Athens, 1951); and Methodios G. Fouyas, *The Social Message of St. John Chrysostom* (privately published, Athens, 1968).

[11]Fouyas, *Social Message*, pp. 101-106.

law both to ameliorate the condition of slaves and then to make it less and less acceptable and viable.[12]

IV. Theological and Ethical Foundations

There is no question that the source of teaching regarding human rights for the Orthodox Church is the fundamental belief that God is the source of all good. Rights arise from the ontological reality of the creation of humanity in the divine image. For Orthodox Christianity, each person and humanity as a whole find their ontological being and reality in the fundamental relationship of the persons of the Holy Trinity. There is an order to the Trinity: the Father is source or *"Arche"*; the Son is eternally born of the Father; the Holy Spirit eternally proceeds from the Father. The interdependence does not minimize the divinity of the persons of the Trinity. Each of the persons is identified by their mutual interrelationship and is differentiated thereby, but, though different in their relationships, each is equally God.

Human rights reflect the triadic or communal pattern of the Trinity. As we relate to others who are created in the divine image, we recognize a common human dignity which, regardless of place or order in society, supplies every person with an ontological status that calls for moral respect. There is an essential and inalienable human equality. As St. Basil affirmed, "By nature every human being has equality according to nature."[13] God has created a commonly shared human nature. Orthodox Christianity's understanding of this natural status is based on the creation of all persons by God in the divine image and according to the divine likeness. In moral situations it is identified as the natural moral law, which, according to the Greek Fathers, is embodied best in the decalogue, but similar embodiments are found in all other religions and cultures.[14]

These moral "oughts" and "ought nots," as we have seen, are reverse statements of human rights, precisely because they are pan-human and universally applicable. Their mutuality is shown in this passage of an early Christian writer, Justin Martyr (100-165):

> God sets before every race of humankind that which is always and universally just, as well as all righteousness; and every race knows that adultery and fornication and homicide and such like are sinful, and though they all commit such practices, yet they do not escape from the knowledge that they act unrighteously when they do so.

[12]Demetropoulos, *E Pistis*, chap. 7, pp. 163-197.

[13]Epistle 262.1.

[14]K. B. Kyriazis, *To Physikon kai to Kanonikon Dikaion ex Epopseos Orthodoxou* (Athens: Apostolike Diakonia, 1957), vols. 1 and 2. Also see Stanley S. Harakas, "The Natural Law Teaching of the Eastern Orthodox Church," *Greek Orthodox Theological Review*, vol. 9, no. 2 (1963-1964), pp. 215-224; reprinted in Martin E. Marty and Dean G. Peerman, eds., *New Theology No. 2* (New York: Macmillan, 1965), pp. 122-133.

. . . For we may see that such persons are unwilling to submit to the same things they inflict upon others, and reproach each other with hostile consciences for the acts which they perpetrate.[15]

At the heart of this Eastern Christian view of natural law is fair and equitable treatment, a right to which all persons appeal on the basis of their humanity. The natural law establishes criteria which, when seen from the perspective of the object of the law's provisions, become rights. "Do not murder" recognizes the right to life. "Do not steal" identifies the right to hold property. "Do not commit adultery" establishes the right to the inviolateness of the marriage relationship, and so on.

Crucial to this theological and ethical grounding is its rootage in God. Secular approaches to rights need to be seen as appeals to a sinful and distorted empirical reality which cannot sustain the claim to rights. Only the appeal to our common origin in God's image and likeness transcends the limited view from below and surely grounds human rights in an unshakable, transcendent truth.

One Greek Orthodox Archbishop has stated the Orthodox position:

> By the term, "dignity of man," no outward and frivolous niceties are implied. Man's need for dignity springs from the very essence of his being. Dignity is the essence of life itself and from it alone is derived the right of man to call himself son of God. Not one of the institutions of man can stand alone without it: whether it be the family, society, the Church, education, or civilization itself. Institutions are to serve people, but if they do not help the individual to be free and to remain free and self-respecting, to feel that he is truly the son of God, the brother of and equal to all others, they do not serve their own purpose. Exploitation, discrimination, social injustice—all are those indomitable forces, characteristic of, but which inevitably bring about the downfall of the reign of the rulers of the darkness of this age.[16]

V. Applications and Development over the Centuries

Undoubtedly human-rights language has become more articulate and pronounced in our times in the Orthodox Church. There is a natural and ready acceptance of human-rights affirmations on the part of the Orthodox Church, as well as a broader application. In the past the rights of nonbelievers, of heretics,

[15]*Dialogue with Trypho*, 93:1-2.
[16]Encyclical of Archbishop Iakovos in *Encyclicals and Documents of the Greek Orthodox Archdiocese of North and South America* (Thessalonica: Patriarchal Institute for Patristic Studies, 1976), pp. 1242-1245. For additional references to human rights in Archbishop Iakovos' encyclicals, see Stanley S. Harakas, "Orthodox Social Conscience, Archbishop Iakovos: A Modern Case," in Demetrios J. Constantelos, ed., *Orthodox Theology and Diakonia: Trends and Prospects* (Brookline, MA: Hellenic College Press, 1981), pp. 193-194.

of minorities, and of women have not been as generally recognized as they are today. Typical of the conflicting views on this matter is the controversy of the Possessors and the Non-Possessors in fifteenth- and sixteenth-century Russia. Regarding, for example, the treatment of heretics, the Possessors "upheld the view all but universal in Christendom at this time: if heretics are recalcitrant, the Church must call in the civil arm and resort to prison, torture, and if necessary fire. But Nilus [spokesperson for the Non-Possessors] condemned all forms of coercion and violence against heretics." The author of these lines commented further, "One has to recall how Protestants and Roman Catholics treated one another in Western Europe during the Reformation, to realize how exceptional Nilus was in his tolerance and respect for human freedom."[17]

Yet, it must also be pointed out that the Non-Possessors did not prevail in seventeenth-, eighteenth-, and nineteenth-century Russia. The strongest claims for human rights during the most recent centuries have been for the right to national and cultural self-determination and for religious freedom. This is understandable, since Orthodox peoples—particularly in the Mediterranean, the Balkans, and the Middle East—for almost four centuries were subject to the Muslim Turkish Ottoman Empire.

The Orthodox Church and the national identities of the Orthodox peoples were closely allied during this period, so it was quite natural for the churches to promote and foster movements of national and cultural self-determination.[18] Sensitivity to individual human aspects of human rights was heightened by the numerous arbitrary acts against Christians by the Turkish overlords, which led to frequent martyrdoms of ordinary people—the neomartyrs.[19] The rise of atheistic and anti-Christian communism in Russia and in other traditionally Orthodox nations since 1917 has sharpened the sensitivity of the Orthodox to religious persecution and to the right to the free exercise of religion.[20]

Consequently, the Orthodox have accepted with remarkable alacrity the 1948 Universal Declaration of Human Rights. The article entitled "The Rights of Human Beings" in the Orthodox *Religious and Ethical Encyclopedia* (Athens) traces the development of the concept from ancient times through Scripture and the patristic period to the U.N. Declaration. The Declaration is "a codification of the specific rules concerning individual freedoms. It proclaims the classical

---

[17]Timothy Ware, *The Orthodox Church* (Baltimore: Penguin Books, 1972), pp. 114-116.

[18]For a history of this period from a perspective of the Ecumenical Patriarchate of Constantinople, see Steven Runciman, *The Great Church in Captivity: A Study of the Patriarchate of Constantinople from the Eve of the Turkish Conquest to the Greek War of Independence* (Cambridge: At the University Press, 1968).

[19]Ioannes E. Anastasiou, "The Neomartyrs of the Greek Orthodox Church," *Alumni Lectures, Number Three* (Brookline, MA: Holy Cross School of Theology, 1973), pp. 89-100.

[20]William B. Stroyen, *Communist Russia and the Russian Orthodox Church* (Washington, DC: Catholic University of America Press, 1967); Paul B. Anderson, *People, Church and State in Modern Russia* (New York: Macmillan, 1944); and the periodicals, *Religion in Communist Dominated Areas* and *The Orthodox Church*.

individual, political and social rights of human beings. . . . It has a supraconstitutional, academic character of orientation for political and social direction."[21] On the thirtieth anniversary of the issuance of the Declaration, the Standing Conference of Canonical Orthodox Bishops in the Americas, representing nine Orthodox Churches in the U.S.A., issued a statement recognizing the value and importance of the Universal Declaration with this exhortation:

> We urge all Orthodox Christians to mark this occasion with prayers for those whose human rights are being denied and/or violated; for those who are harassed and persecuted because of their religious beliefs, Orthodox and non-Orthodox alike, in many parts of the world; for those whose rightful demands and persistence are met with greater oppression and ignominy; and for those whose agony for justice, food, shelter, health care and education is accelerated with each passing day.

> We ask that you support President Carter's request that the Senate approve the United Nations International Covenants on Economic, Social and Cultural Rights, and on Civil and Political Rights, as recorded in the Universal Declaration of Human Rights.[22]

Further developments have occurred. For example, the Greek Orthodox Archdiocese of North and South America has repeatedly adopted human-rights statements at its Clergy-Laity Congresses.[23] At its Clergy-Laity Congress in 1980, it decried both the persecution of the Orthodox minority in Turkey and the armed occupation of Cyprus with its violation of human rights. It issued a resolution, as well, on "Human and Religious Rights," which said in part:

> WHEREAS, the United Nations Charter, the United Nations Declaration of Human Rights, the European Commission on Human Rights, the Helsinki Accord and other internationally accepted documents recognize the basic human rights of all people; and

> WHEREAS, human rights consist of those conditions of life that allow us fully to develop and use our human qualities of intelligence and conscience to their fullest extent and to satisfy our spiritual, social and political needs, including freedom of expression, freedom from fear, harassment, intimidation and discrimination and freedom to participate in the functions of government and to have the guarantee of the equal protection of law; and

---

[21]*Threskevtike kai Ethike Engkyklopaideia* (Athens: Athan Martinos Publishers, 1964), vol. 4, pp. 1218-1221.

[22]Archdiocesan Archives. Issued December, 1978, and promulgated in the Greek Orthodox Archdiocese by a cover encyclical.

[23]For the texts of these human-rights statements, see my forthcoming book (to be published by Light and Life Publishing Co., Minneapolis), "Contemporary Moral Issues Facing the Orthodox Christian," especially chaps. 33, "Human Rights"; 34, "Equal Rights"; and 35, "Are Orthodox Christians Racist?"

WHEREAS, the policies and actions of certain governments of the world, whether through hypocritically subtle means or overt manifestations of systematic repression, have violated these basic human rights; and

WHEREAS, it is a shame and stigma for 20th century civilization that there are nations which, through insecurity resort to practices of the dark ages by holding hostages and that there are ruthless regimes which, by imposing indescribable suffering upon minorities living within their borders, force them to abandon their ancestral homes, which declare free citizens persona non grata, which forcibly prevent the free emigration of citizens seeking to leave, and which ostracize some as political exiles; and

WHEREAS, it is the moral and social responsibility and obligation of the free and democratic nations of this world to not only condemn and disavow such violations wherever they occur, but to take such affirmative steps as will restore realization of these inherent rights and a true respect thereof.

NOW, THEREFORE, BE IT RESOLVED by the 25th Clergy-Laity Congress of the Greek Orthodox Archdiocese of North and South America that we call upon totalitarian and oppressive regimes to restore respect for the rights and dignity of the individual and to insure the free and unhindered exercise of these vital rights by all citizens, regardless of racial or ethnic origin, or political or religious espousal; and

BE IT FURTHER RESOLVED that we call upon all free and democratic governments of the world, and in particular the United States of America, to exercise their moral and political responsibilities for the preservation of human rights by adoption of clear, concise and consistent policies, both domestic and foreign, reflective of these fundamental human rights.[24]

Similar statements on human rights with particular reference to the Middle East situation have been issued by the Antiochian Archdiocese.[25]

The Orthodox Church in America (formerly the Russian Orthodox Greek Catholic Church in America) has also made statements on human rights with special focus on the violation of human rights in the Soviet Union—especially the freedom of religion.[26]

---

[24]*Minutes, Decisions, Resolutions and Statements of the 25th Clergy-Laity Congress of the Greek Orthodox Archdiocese of North and South America in Atlanta, Georgia, June 27-July 5, 1980*, pp. 114-115.

[25]"The Minutes of the General Assembly of the XXXV Convention of the Antiochian Orthodox Christian Archdiocese of North and South America," published in *The Word* 25 (November, 1981), included resolutions on Lebanon, "The Rights of Arab Christians and Muslims in Israel," "Palestinian National and Human Rights," and for "a comprehensive resolution of the Palestinian-Israeli conflict," pp. 24-26.

[26]Repeated and detailed accounts of human and religious rights, violations, encyclicals,

This progress in the sharper formulation of human rights is good. But there is need for the Orthodox Church to universalize its witness for human rights. This is precisely one of the goals of the forthcoming Great and Holy Council of the Orthodox Church. Long in preparation, the tenth of the ten agenda items adopted includes several items of social concern, including "freedom and brotherhood." In a brief introduction to these topics the challenge of the future on such issues was outlined:

> It would seem that the Great and Holy Council of the Orthodox Church has an important and creative task to perform regarding the development of a consistent, theologically sound Orthodox Christian Social Ethic. However, it must not merely exhort to more study, alone. It is time for the Orthodox Church to reassume its prophetic role and speak out to the issues. Further, guidelines for action need to be articulated or encouraged. This is the golden opportunity for Orthodoxy to return to its grand tradition of love for humanity at large, not only in word and prayer, but in concerted action as well.[27]

These views also are readily applicable to the issue of human rights.

Other issues are equally in need of study and report. In the field of bio-ethics, for instance, patient rights, prenatal rights, and the rights of the dying have only begun to be treated by the Orthodox, as have questions pertaining to women's rights.

VI. The Basis for Interfaith Dialogue on Human Rights

In an article on ethics in an ecumenical perspective,[28] I argued that ethics cannot be the starting point or even a major contributor to inter-church dialogue, because, for Eastern Orthodoxy, ethics is a derivative discipline, dependent for its first principles on the truths of doctrine. It is a long-standing Orthodox view that true Christian unity cannot be achieved without genuine agreement on the major and chief doctrinal matters. Yet, that same article expressed the view that there are areas of cooperation open to the various traditions of ethics within Christianity. "In the practical area of ecumenical relations, it appears that what is now occurring will continue to be the practice, i. e., Christians of varying backgrounds will work in *ad hoc* alliances on single issues. For them, these will be ecumenical experiences. Unfortunately, it is very likely

---

and Sober decisions on topics such as this are found in almost every issue of *The Orthodox Church*, the official monthly newspaper of the Orthodox Church in America.

[27]Stanley S. Harakas, *Something Is Stirring in World Orthodoxy: An Introduction to the Forthcoming Great and Holy Council of the Orthodox Church* (Minneapolis: Light and Life Publishing Co., 1978), p. 66.

[28]"Christian Ethics in Ecumenical Perspective: An Orthodox Christian View," *Journal of Ecumenical Studies* 15 (1978): 631-646.

that other Christians will be ranged against them in their own ecumenical *ad hoc* alliances!"[29]

One of the most promising areas, however, for ecumenical cooperation in both dialogue and principle agreement, as well as in concerted ecumenical action, is the issue of human rights. If, as we have seen, the Orthodox are able to endorse statements on human rights such as the U.N. Declaration and the Helsinki Accords, which are essentially secular documents (given what has been said above about theological agreement), there must be a realistic hope that ecumenical consensus on the question of human rights can be achieved in some measure.[30] However, it seems to me that agreement in broad, general principle will be easier than coming to cases and adjudicating them on the basis of these principles. The conflicts of Cypriot Greeks and Turks, of Palestinian Arabs (both Christian and Muslim) and Israeli Jews, and of Protestants and Roman Catholics in Ireland will not be analyzed with the same objectivity.

But the effort must be made. It would seem that in these and so many other cases in which all parties claim violation of their human rights the role of Christian ethics can be a force for the recognition of the justice of conflicting human rights claims (where they be such). Further, Christian ethics can seek to contribute to the adoption of a conciliatory spirit which may serve to resolve the tensions of these conflicting human rights claims. I am not optimistic that the power forces and the heightened passions involved in each of these conflicts can easily be directed into the paths of peace and justice, but certainly it is the kind of course to which the discipline of ethics will wish to contribute.

---

[29]Ibid., p. 644.

[30]For a less enthusiastic assessment of the U.N. Charter from an Evangelical Protestant perspective, see Ronald H. Nash, "Rights," in Carl F. H. Henry, ed., *Baker's Dictionary of Christian Ethics* (Washington, DC: Canon Press, 1973), pp. 589-591.

3.

HUMAN RIGHTS IN ROMAN CATHOLICISM

John Langan

I

The central and classical document for the doctrine of human rights in the Roman Catholic tradition is *Pacem in terris* (Peace on Earth), the encyclical letter which Pope John XXIII issued in 1963. It represents a moment of equipoise, of creative assimilation and synthesis, which comes after a long period of struggle and tension but which in turn gives rise to further questions and challenges, many of them unforeseen and unintended by the fashioners of the synthesis. *Pacem in terris*, together with the decrees of Vatican II, is the resolution of a crucial stage of Roman Catholicism's long struggle with the modernizing and secularizing culture of the West. In this stuggle the issue of religious freedom was central, but the notion of human rights included a much wider range of concerns than simply religious freedom, and it provided a basis for the transformation of Catholicism from an ally and ward of traditionalist regimes to a critic of repression by both reactionary and revolutionary regimes.

Pacem in terris proceeds in a serene and irenic manner which conceals much of the struggle that raged during the preceding 200 years on both the philosophical-theological and the social-political fronts. John XXIII began with the necessity of human rights for the good order of society: "Any human society, if it is to be well-ordered and productive, must lay down as a foundation this principle, namely, that every human being is a person, that is, his nature is endowed with intelligence and free will. By virtue of this, he has rights and duties, flowing directly and simultaneously from his very nature. These rights are therefore universal, inviolable and inalienable."[1] This passage reveals a great deal about the standard form of Catholic human-rights theory as it is presented in the official social teaching of the Church.

First, it employs two key notions which are presented as harmonizing with each other, namely, the personal character of the human being manifested in intelligence and freedom, and the nature which is the source of rights and duties. This combination of two different patterns of thinking about humanity distinguishes the Catholic tradition from those forms of idealism and existentialism

---

[1]John XXIII, *Pacem in terris/Peace on Earth* (New York: America Press, 1963), par. 9.

John P. Langan (Roman Catholic), a Jesuit priest, is a Research Fellow at the Woodstock Theological Center at Georgetown University in Washington, DC. He received his doctorate in philosophy from the University of Michigan. Author of numerous articles in the area of ethics and social justice, he is co-editor (with Alfred Hennelly) of and a contributor to *Human Rights in the Americas: The Struggle for Consensus*.

26

which set a fundamental distinction between the realm of natural law and the realm of personal freedom, and also from those tendencies in the empiricist and positivist traditions which would reduce the personal to the natural interpreted as the scientifically knowable. Human-rights theory in Catholicism works from an anthropology which is fundamentally realistic in its account of human knowing and of human moral endeavor and which stresses both the unity of the human person as a being in the world and the necessary orientation of the person to society and community. This anthropology is compatible with and takes inspiration from such central Christian theological doctrines as the Incarnation and the creation of human beings "in the image and likeness of God" (Gen. 1:26),[2] but it is not presented as accessible only to those who accept these theological beliefs. It is nourished by the Christian view of the unfolding of salvation in history and by the more specifically Catholic sense of the ecclesial community as one in space and time and by the Catholic form of sacramental imagination.[3] As a result, Catholic proponents of this anthropology and its application to human rights will often seem most distinctively Catholic to those who come from other religious and intellectual traditions when they take themselves to be simply delineating the contours of the universally human.

Second, the doctrine aims to be universal and not particularistic in both its foundation and its application.[4] The foundation of human rights and of the principles of order for human society generally is to be found "where the Father of all things wrote them, that is, in the nature of man."[5] The role of divinely revealed truth in discovering these norms is essentially confirmatory.[6] The basing of human rights on natural law provides a link with the central Catholic theological tradition, particularly Thomas Aquinas; it also provides a parallel to the move made by Western revolutionaries in the eighteenth century in appealing beyond the complexities, irrationalities, and injustices of positive law and the institutions of the old regime to a "higher law," which affirmed natural and God-given rights. The desire for a foundation for human rights which would be universally accessible is also interwoven with the contemporary desire of the Church to address the modern world in its own terms.[7] But it may be doubted whether a natural-law foundation for human rights really enhances communication with either secular liberals or Reformed Christians. A very good case can be made that

---

[2]Ibid., par. 3.

[3]For a presentation of the relevance of sacramental imagination to issues of social justice, see David Hollenbach, "A Prophetic Church and the Catholic Sacramental Imagination," in John Haughey, ed., *The Faith That Does Justice* (New York: Paulist, 1977).

[4]The formulation of human-rights doctrine in the standard English translation of *Pacem in terris* used here may seem to go against this claim and to be particularistic in an objectionable way, i.e., sexist. This problem of formulation (as contrasted with possible problems of content) arises from the English translation and not from the official Latin version.

[5]John XXIII, *Pacem in terris*, par. 6.

[6]Ibid., par. 10.

[7]This desire is manifest particularly in *Gaudium et spes*, the constitution of Vatican II on the Church and the Modern World (1965).

the appeal of human rights norms themselves is really far broader than the appeal of any philosophical or theological foundation which may be offered for them.[8] Thus there has been a tendency in more recent Catholic teaching to put less explicit reliance on natural-law categories, even though there is no sharp change in the underlying anthropology. This tendency is also, in part, a consequence of the desire to present more of the Church's teaching in biblical terms.

The universality envisaged in Catholicism's approach to human rights also involves the range of application of such claims. Thus *Pacem in terris*, as we have seen, affirms that human rights are "universal, inviolable, and inalienable."[9] These are to be protected by law,[10] and special programs to ensure the rights of "the less fortunate members of the community," who are "less able to defend their rights," are commended by the encyclical.[11] John XXIII explicitly noted the increasing participation of women in public life and their growing sense of their human dignity which impelled them to claim "the rights and duties that befit a human person."[12] He also affirmed the equality of all human beings "by reason of their natural dignity" and argued from this that racial discrimination cannot be justified[13] and that all political communities have equal natural dignity.[14] Neither sex nor race nor economic class can, then, form a basis for denying or restricting the rights of human persons.

Human rights not only apply to all groups, even those most oppressed in the past, but they are also moral claims which are more binding than the enactments of states. Thus, John XXIII held that "if any government does not acknowledge the rights of man or violates them, it not only fails in its duty, but its orders completely lack juridical force."[15] It is important, however, to note that here he did not accept interpretations of universal human rights which would overturn such customary institutions of Western society as the family, the private ownership of property, the nation-states, and ethnic communities.[16] In the papal approach, rights claims are normally advanced within an ongoing framework of social institutions. These institutions are obliged to respect and promote human rights in various ways, but the destruction or enfeebling of these institutions would serve neither the common good nor, in the long run, the cause of human rights. There is room, then, for considerations which might justify the restriction or overriding of human rights claims, even though the details of such justifica-

---

[8]Foundational proposals, however, retain the values of showing ways to integrate human-rights norms into the various religious, intellectual, and political traditions and of clarifying their relationship to major philosophical and theological issues. Evidence for the greater appeal of human-rights norms independent of foundations can be seen in the Universal Declaration of Human Rights itself, which makes no foundational claim; in the near-universal reluctance of governments of all ideological hues to admit that they violate human rights; and in the general public response to the work of Amnesty International and similar organizations.

[9]John XXIII, *Pacem in terris*, par. 9.   [13]Ibid., par. 44.
[10]Ibid., par. 79.   [14]Ibid., par. 89.
[11]Ibid., par. 56.   [15]Ibid., par. 61.
[12]Ibid., par. 41.   [16]See ibid., pars. 16, 21, 48, 55, 92, 100.

28

tion are not worked out. The encyclical does not attempt to prescribe one particular form or constitution for states on the basis of human rights considerations.[17] It acknowledges the diversity of historical circumstances but strongly commends both the separation of powers and the advantages of citizen participation in government.[18]

Third, the content of human-rights doctrine in *Pacem in terris* is comprehensive. The encyclical gives what David Hollenbach in his valuable study of the Catholic human rights tradition, *Claims in Conflict*, called "the most complete and systematic list of . . . human rights in the modern Catholic tradition."[19] It includes both what are commonly referred to as civil and political rights (of the sort listed in Articles 1-21 of the Universal Declaration of Human Rights[20] and social and economic rights (Articles 22-28 of the Universal Declaration), but it does not enumerate rights on the basis of this common but often perplexing categorization. The encyclical also offers an explicit, though qualified, endorsement of the Universal Declaration of Human Rights, which it calls "an important step on the path toward the juridico-political organization of the world community,"[21] precisely because of its acknowledgment of the dignity of all human persons.

The encyclical consciously juxtaposes items from different ideological traditions in its enumeration of rights. Thus it lays down as the starting point of its enumeration "the right to life, to bodily integrity, and to the means which are necessary and suitable for the proper development of life"; these means include "food, clothing, shelter, rest, medical care, and finally the necessary social services."[22] The position laid down in this one paragraph can be appealed to in criticism both of regimes which practice judicial murder and the "disappearance" of dissidents and of societies which fail to provide the things necessary for the survival for all their members. So, also, when John XXIII spoke of rights within the economic sphere, he affirmed that "human beings have the natural right to free initiative in the economic field and the right to work."[23] Here he picked up the concern of liberal capitalism for promoting freedom of entrepreneurial activity, the free disposition of private property, and freedom of choice in market situations, even while he also endorsed the obligation affirmed by socialist and social democratic movements of providing all citizens with an opportunity to exercise their right to work. These juxtapositions illustrate the tendency in the major documents of the church's social teaching to find a middle way between laissez-faire capitalism and Marxist socialism.

---

[17]Ibid., par. 67.
[18]Ibid., pars. 68, 74.
[19]David Hollenbach, *Claims in Conflict: Retrieving and Renewing the Catholic Human Rights Tradition* (New York: Paulist Press, 1979), p. 66.
[20]See pp. 105-109, below.
[21]John XXIII, *Pacem in terris*, par. 144.
[22]Ibid., par. 11.
[23]Ibid., par. 18.

A fourth characteristic tendency of Catholic presentations of human-rights doctrine is the concern for moral and religious values. *Pacem in terris* includes a strong affirmation of the right of human beings to "honor God according to the dictates of an upright conscience" and to profess one's "religion privately and publicly."[24] This affirmation is still based on our obligation to serve God rightly and on the church's right to liberty; in some respects it falls short of the formulation employed by Vatican II in its declaration on religious freedom, which holds that, even in cases where there is an establishment or special legal recognition of one form of religion, "it is at the same time imperative that the right of all citizens and religious bodies should be recognized and made effective in practice."[25] Part of what is being worked out in *Pacem in terris* is the problem of reconciling the rights to freedom of belief and expression with the obligatory aspects of such values as truth, the common good, and the moral virtues— a problem which continues to trouble liberal democracies.[26]

What the Catholic tradition was able to do in the discussion of religious liberty leading up to Vatican II was to work out a nonrelativistic, nonagnostic foundation for religious freedom. In this approach, the human obligation to seek truth in religious matters is to be understood in accordance with the "dignity of the human person and his social nature";[27] it is, therefore, to be free and dialogical. Vatican II was then able to affirm the obligation to follow conscience and to respect both conscience in others and, what had often been in practice the more difficult point, the right of religious groups to be constituted, to gather, and to worship in public and private. The council also argued for religious freedom on the basis of the freedom of the act of faith and contended that respect for religious freedom was in accordance with the example and teaching of Jesus.[28]

Pacem in terris manifests the concern of the Catholic human-rights tradition to set specific rights into a moral context which includes, in addition to the distinct values of truth and the moral virtues, the more immediately linked network of rights and duties, both those attaching to the person who is the subject of a particular right and those attaching to other persons who may affect or be affected by the subject's exercise of her or his right. This concern is generalized in the two principles of the correlation of rights and duties in the individual subject and between persons. John XXIII illustrated the first type of correlation with the following examples: "The right of every man to life is correlative with the duty to preserve it; his right to a decent standard of living,

---

[24]Ibid., par. 14.
[25]Vatican II, Declaration on Religious Freedom, *Dignitatis humanae*, par. 6.
[26]The current wave of controversy in the Unites States over such disparate "moral" issues as pornography, school prayers, and abortion can serve as evidence of both continued dissatisfaction with the form of liberalism dominant in the juridical system and of the difficulty of stating the issues in a form acceptable to both sides in the disputes.
[27]Vatican II, *Dignitatis humanae*, par. 3.
[28]Ibid., pars. 10, 11.

with the duty of living it becomingly; and his right to investigate the truth freely, with the duty of pursuing it ever more completely and profoundly."[29] The basis of this first correlation of rights and duties is a recognition that the goods with which both are concerned are essential to human flourishing and are, at least in their most fundamental and universal forms, not optional for human beings.[30] The consequence of this first correlation is that the individual is not in a condition of pure liberty and discretion with regard to these goods but remains under moral obligation. There is not, once this correlation is granted, a simple division between freedom and law as Hobbes supposed in his remark that "Law and Right differ as much as Obligation and Liberty; which in one and the same matter are inconsistent."[31]

The second correlation which is proposed is the more familiar one that obtains between persons: "To one man's natural right there corresponds a duty in other persons: the duty, namely, of acknowledging and respecting the right in question."[32] Those who claim rights for themselves without acknowledging the rights of others are guilty of a fundamental inconsistency. The practice of claiming and exercising rights is not merely an instrument for protecting and advancing self-interest, though it can be that, but it can itself be obligatory as an expression of respect for one's human dignity. John XXIII wrote, "He who possesses certain rights has likewise the duty to claim those rights."[33] This clearly is not intended to rule out all cases of waiving one's rights, but it makes a point against sacrificial conceptions of Christian morality.

The mutual acknowledgment of rights and duties in society is also seen as a kind of *preparatio evangelica*, since it brings human beings to awareness of a world of values such as "truth, justice, charity, and freedom" and brings them to "a better knowledge of the true God, who is personal and transcendent."[34] Here one finds the possibility of a political theology which takes as its starting point not the struggle of the oppressed in a radically unjust society, but the active involvement of persons in exercising rights and fulfilling duties in a society which provides at least the possibility of meeting the demands of justice and attaining the common good through its institutions and practices. There is positive religious value in the advancing and weighing of claims, in the organization and advocacy of groups of citizens working for a cause, and in the characteristic activities of a society which is participatory rather than hierarchical in its understanding of order and fulfillment. This marks a large and important shift in Catholicism's vision of human society.

In summary, the Roman Catholic understanding of human rights in its

[29]John XXIII, *Pacem in terris*, par. 29.
[30]See John Finnis, *Natural Law and Natural Rights* (New York: Oxford University Press, 1980).
[31]Thomas Hobbes, *Leviathan*, ed. C. B. Macpherson (Baltimore: Penguin, 1968), p. 189.
[32]John XXIII, *Pacem in terris*, par. 30.
[33]Ibid., par. 44.
[34]Ibid., par. 45.

classical form differs from the dominant varieties of liberalism, especially in Anglo-American culture, in its distrust of individualism and its emphasis on community. This is a matter of both the underlying anthropology and the moral restraints that affect the exercise of freedom in society. It differs from Protestant approaches in its mode of argumentation and presentation, which relies on philosophical rather than theological or biblical categories in dealing with basic issues of political and legal theory. Catholic human-rights doctrine emerges as a comprehensive and generous structure within which religious believers can both share and address the moral dilemmas of a religiously pluralistic and increasingly secular world and which, while not without some internal points of tension and incompleteness, is able to offer shelter to those who are repelled both by the neglect of social and economic rights for the disadvantaged in liberal societies and by the repressiveness of authoritarian and totalitarian regimes. But it would be misleading to look at the Catholic human-rights tradition only in its classical moment of synthesis. It is necessary to look both backward to the struggles of its past and forward to the potentialities and problems of its future.

II

If one moves back 100 years before *Pacem in terris* in the history of papal teaching on society, one comes to the *Syllabus of Errors* of Pius IX (1864). Among the positions *condemned* in this celebrated list are the following:

55. The Church should be separated from the State and the State from the Church.

77. In this age of ours it is no longer expedient that the Catholic religion should be treated as the sole State religion and that any other forms of religious worship should be excluded.

78. Hence those States, nominally Catholic, who have legally enacted that immigrants be permitted to have free exercise of their own particular religion, are to be praised.[35]

Pius IX was struggling to preserve a privileged or even a monopoly position for the Catholic religion. In so doing, he was continuing the opposition to religious freedom which Pius VI, in the face of the French Revolution's Declaration of the Rights of Man, had enunciated as early as the brief *Quod aliquantum* of 1791, which singled out for criticism the articles calling for freedom of opinion and communication.[36] Catholicism's institutional sympathies during most of the

[35]Pius IX, *Syllabus of Errors*, in *Church and State through the Centuries*, trans. and ed. Sidney Ehler and John Morrall (London: Burns and Oates, 1954), pp. 284-285.
[36]See Bernard Plongeron, "Anathema or Dialogue? Christian Reactions to Declarations of the Rights of Man in the United States and Europe in the Eighteenth Century," trans. Lawrence Ginn, in *The Church and the Rights of Man*, Concilium 124, ed. Alois Muller and Norbert Greinacher (New York: Seabury, 1979), p. 41.

nineteenth century were with a conservatism which had its roots in the *ancien regime*. It is important neither to conceal nor to overstate these sympathies. The Church, especially in France, experienced the proclamation of human rights in 1789 as a very cold and hostile wind, and it cannot claim for itself a significant place in either the theoretical or the practical struggle for human rights in the eighteenth and nineteenth centuries. Human-rights theory in an explicit and politically dynamic form confronted Catholicism as an alien force, and it has taken Catholicism a long time to appropriate it.

If it is true, as Wolfgang Huber has argued, that "the consciousness of human rights arose in the context of confrontation with the principle of absolute sovereignty,"[37] it has to be recognized that the church, even in its most conservative and supine phase, always felt the responsibility to oppose the principle of absolute sovereignty, whether exercised by Louis XIV or Napoleon. The necessity of this opposition arises from the church's concern for its own liberty in proclaiming the gospel, in carrying on its sacramental life, and in ordering its communities. Catholicism gave a convinced but not unconditional support to the old order, a support which was reinforced by the anti-clericalism of many proponents of the new doctrines. The Church feared for its privileged position and its property, but also for its place in the hearts of the faithful and its freedom to be itself. This fear was naturally greatest where the Church had most to lose (that is, the traditionally Catholic lands of Europe and Latin America), and least strong where the Church had adjusted to competitive or even repressive conditions (as in North America, Holland, Ireland, and Poland).[38] Catholicism has always had the intellectual and moral instruments (if not the political will or courage) to condemn the gorier excesses of tyranny and barbarism, which are at the same time violations of human rights. The major exceptions to this have also involved the denial of religious freedom, as in various crusading and inquisitorial activities.

The first stage in the development of Catholic human-rights doctrine can be located in the reign of Pius IX's successor, Leo XIII, who, in 1891, issued his famous encyclical on the condition of the working class in industrial society, *Rerum novarum*. Along with a vehement affirmation of the natural rights of property[39] and a denunciation of the Marxist notion of class struggle,[40] Leo affirmed "the natural right" of each person "to procure what is required in order to live."[41] Leo XIII himself used this as part of his argument for a just or living wage and against an unrestricted freedom of contract between employers and

---

[37]Wolfgang Huber, "Human Rights—A Concept and Its History" in *The Church and the Rights of Man*, trans. Martin Kitchen, Concilium 124, p. 5.

[38]Plongeron, in "Anathema," pp. 40-42, makes this point specifically for the period of immediate reactions to the French Revolution, but I think it is more generally relevant.

[39]Leo XIII, *Rerum novarum*, pars. 5-10.

[40]Ibid., pars. 15-17.

[41]Ibid., par. 34. In taking this position, Leo XIII was following the teaching of Thomas Aquinas, *Summa Theologiae*, II-II, 66,7.

workers. But we can also see this as the nucleus of a theory of subsistence rights, that is, social and economic rights to those things which are necessary for survival. These rights are prior to any particular political, legal, or economic order: "Man precedes the State, and possesses, prior to the formation of any State, the right of providing for the sustenance of his body."[42] Hollenbach observed that Leo's stress on the primacy of the personal was more creative for the Catholic Church's teachings on economic rights than in the political and cultural spheres, where Leo continued "the classical association of Catholic thought with a hierarchical and traditionalist model of social organization."[43] The papacy was, in fact, more ready to challenge economic liberalism and the practices of laissez-faire capitalism than to endorse egalitarian democracy.

The second stage is not marked by one central document but consists in Catholicism's acceptance of the values, procedures, and norms of Western constitutional democracy as the appropriate framework for modern societies. This is the result of a painful process of learning from the great European civil war of 1914 to 1945 and its aftermath in the Cold War. Put simply, it is the church's movement from the time of Franz Josef to the time of Konrad Adenauer, through the time of Adolf Hitler. During this period the last hopes for a return to the values and practices of the old regime were destroyed; the evils of racism and totalitarianism were made manifest on a colossal scale; and the Western constitutional democracies emerged as relatively humane victors and as the de facto protectors of Catholicism against communist advances in Europe.

Two aspects of this process should be mentioned, one practical and the other theoretical. The first is the emergence of Christian Democratic parties which gave the church and the world an experience and an example of political life that was both religious and democratic and that could be trusted with the exercise of power in ways which did not infringe on human rights. The second is the work of Jacques Maritain in developing from Thomistic foundations an understanding of natural law and the common good which included as a vital and constitutive element the rights of the human person.[44] This was an important reaction to totalitarian ways of interpreting common good which would allow the destruction of persons for the sake of preserving or enhancing the power of the state.

The end of this second phase of Catholic development coincided with the internationalization and universalization of human rights in the declarations of the Allies, in the moral reflections provoked by the war-crimes trials, and ultimately in the Universal Declaration of Human Rights in 1948. It also coincided with the decisive beginnings of the process of decolonization in Asia and with

---

[42]Leo XIII, *Rerum novarum*, par. 6.

[43]Hollenbach, *Claims in Conflict*, p. 49.

[44]See especially his works of the war and post-war years: *The Rights of Man and Natural Law*, trans. Doris Anson (New York: Scribner's, 1945); *The Person and the Common Good*, trans. John Fitzgerald (New York: Scribner's, 1947); and *Man and the State* (Chicago: The University of Chicago Press, 1951).

the move to universal application of the Wilsonian principle of national self-determination. These processes meant the end of Western hegemony over the non-European world and opened the way for a less Eurocentric way of conceiving both human rights and Catholicism, which became manifest in Vatican II and in the social teaching of Paul VI with its focus on problems of development. One very important aftermath of the global extension of the notion of human rights and of greater realization of the evils of racism was that the struggle for human rights took as one of its central and paradigmatic forms the struggle against discrimination.

The third phase of the development we have already seen in *Pacem in terris* and in Vatican Council II. With regard to religious liberty, the church found considerable difficulty in accepting human-rights norms which had formed part of enlightened opinion since the late eighteenth century. Whereas the affirmation of most human rights is a lesson which the church teaches its faithful and the world, the affirmation of religious freedom is a lesson which the church itself must learn. The church even in its modernized form is more comfortable in conceiving itself as a moral teacher proposing norms than as a moral agent whose actions are to be bound by norms. The eventual acceptance of the principle of religious freedom owed much to the experience of Catholicism in the United States and to the theological work of John Courtney Murray, S.J., in explicating that experience in terms which did not imply relativistic indifferentism or secularism.[45] What was required was not merely a theoretical argument, but also an encouraging example of Catholicism flourishing in an open society, an example which could overcome the fears and the defensiveness shown by the church in earlier phases of human-rights development. The decisive removal of equivocation on the issue of religious freedom by Vatican II was a major, though belated, accomplishment which both preserved the credibility of the Catholic Church's teaching on human rights and opened the way to fuller and richer relationships with other religious traditions.

III

Few major accomplishments, however, are without problematic consequences. Few syntheses remain unchallenged; few classic moments are undisturbed. Let us then look, briefly, at the relatively recent past since the end of Vatican II in 1965 and at the challenges of the near future. There are, I suggest, four of these which bear watching.

First, there are still unresolved elements in the church's struggle with modern individualism and liberalism. At a fairly deep level within Catholicism there lives a desire for a more unified, more cohesive, and more disciplined form

---

[45]John Courtney Murray, *We Hold These Truths* (New York: Sheed and Ward, 1960).

of society than prevails in the secularized West. There is also a view that liberalism errs in giving too much room to individual freedom at the expense of the common good and the needs of the disadvantaged, that its doctrine of rights leads to a neglect of duties, that liberal societies have lapsed into a resentful and self-protective consumerism, and that liberalism involves both the denial of a normative structure of goods for human beings in society and serious errors in anthropology. All this is, of course, apt material for future debate and dialogue. It does not indicate that Catholicism will abandon its human-rights doctrine; the doctrine now has the weight of authority and argument behind it. But it does indicate that institutional Catholicism and Catholic political movements and actors may make significantly different choices about which human rights to struggle for in the political arena and which rights to accord priority to. One manifest example of this is the characteristically but not exclusively Roman Catholic concern for the right to life of the unborn. Catholic human-rights theorizing and advocacy will probably continue to be distinctively Catholic, even as they attempt to grasp the contours of the universally human and natural.

Second, there is an unresolved question about the preferred shape of society from the standpoint of human-rights theory. If one espouses a comprehensive human-rights theory including both civil and political rights and social and economic rights, as Catholicism does, what form of economy and polity will enable a society to meet this complex set of moral demands and constraints? This question is directly related to Catholicism's search for a middle way between Marxist socialism and what John Paul II calls "rigid capitalism."[46] Certain answers are clear. The state must acknowledge the rule of law. Its power must be limited, not absolute. It must respect the right to life and religious freedom. This rules out both communist regimes and national security states of the type which have developed in the Southern Cone of Latin America since 1964. The promise of liberal democracies with regulated capitalist economies to satisfy social and economic rights is weak, and their performance is uneven. But the record of professedly socialist societies with regard to both social and economic rights and civil and political rights is discouraging. Some form of social democracy or of chastened and humanized socialism seems to be indicated.

But this is a long way from giving a concrete answer to the basic question about the preferred shape of the future society, an answer which might motivate political action and guide political choices. It is a basic limitation of human-rights theory that it is more helpful in enabling us to denounce violations of human dignity than in guiding us in the design of institutions which will promote that dignity.[47] However, efforts to enlarge human-rights theory to deal with fundamental questions of political and economic order and to provide the basis

---

[46]John Paul II, *Laborem exercens*, par. 14.
[47]One interesting effort to move beyond this limited result in the direction of normative principles for policy is found in Hollenbach, *Claims in Conflict*, chap. 5, especially pp. 195-207.

36

for a political program run the double risk of breaking the moral consensus about human-rights violations which is capable of transcending standard political and ideological divisions and of producing an overly moralistic and legalistic approach which may be inappropriate to the deeper problems of economic development and world order.

Third, there is the question of a shifting foundation for Catholic human-rights theory. In the key documents of the 1960's, particularly *Pacem in terris* and *Gaudium et spes*, which is Vatican II's pastoral constitution on the church and the modern world, there is a polarity between neo-scholastic and biblical approaches to the bases of Christian human rights, between what Hollenbach called "universalist and particularist warrants for human rights theory."[48] He noted the turn away from a rationalistic neo-scholastic philosophical approach on the basis of natural law to a more flexible theological approach which is sensitive to the processes of history and the diversity of cultures. This is simply one aspect of the general movement in contemporary Catholicism away from the once dominant and mandatory system of neo-Thomism.

While the turn to a more biblical and less *a priori* approach to human-rights theory creates new possibilities for dialogue with other religious traditions, especially Protestantism, it leaves a gap between the historical and theological categories of biblical revelation and the philosophical, legal, and practical categories of human-rights theory and action. This gap is not particularly difficult to overcome when it is a matter of appealing to religious symbols in order to motivate. But the difficult questions of the weight and interconnection of different types of rights and the necessity of collaborative work and reflection with secularists and people of radically different religious traditions mean that some systematic positions in ethics, political philosophy, and jurisprudence will have to be brought back into the argument, smuggled in under cover of theological darkness. I have already argued both that the anthropological basis is essential to the elaboration of Catholic human-rights theory and that it cannot be divided neatly into philosophical and theological segments. However, the recognition of the importance of historical process and cultural diversity is an important corrective to premature rationalistic systematizations of the sort that neo-scholastic philosophy was only too ready to perpetrate.[49] One happy byproduct of this double foundation for human-rights theory in Catholicism is the opportunity it creates for a wider range of dialogue with people from a diversity of religious and intellectual traditions.

A fourth area of future challenge and development is to be found in the internal life of Roman Catholicism itself. The Church uses human-rights doctrine to proclaim a message of justice and peace to the world, but the applicability of

---

[48]Hollenbach has an excellent treatment of this polarity in relation to secular philosophical and Protestant styles of ethical theory in his *Claims in Conflict*, pp. 108-118.

[49]For some telling conservative criticisms of the misuse of the concept of nature in later scholastic moral theory, see Finnis, *Natural Law*, p. 102.

the doctrine to the Church itself remains unclear.[50] Thus, there is no significant use of human-rights doctrine in the proposed revision of the Code of Canon Law. But the problems are more extensive and more troubling than this lacuna suggests. For it has been argued that rights to participation and to self-determination on the part of the laity are not effectively exercised and protected, that the exclusion of women from ordained ministry and from most positions of power in the Catholic Church is a discriminatory violation of rights to equal treatment and equal respect, that ordained ministers are denied the right to marry, that theologians are restricted in their rights to freedom of inquiry and expression, that lay employees of the Church are often denied rights to organization and to social benefits, and that due process procedures for the protection of rights are weak or nonexistent.[51]

Not all these issues are "live" issues in all parts of the Catholic Church; in fact, the list just given reflects characteristic concerns of North Atlantic Catholicism, particularly those parts of it influenced by Anglo-American legal culture. This is the heartland of human-rights theory, and so its concerns, while not universal, are particularly revealing. One should also note the different character of the different issues. Some involve matters of theological principle (e.g., the ordination of women), or fundamentals of church discipline (e.g., marriage of the clergy and modes of lay participation). Some involve more-or-less widespread abuses (e.g., denial of the right to form unions). Some may involve both. It seems to me unfair and unwise to treat those who have honest disagreements on matters of principle as favoring either the violation of human rights or the overthrow of church discipline.

There are three main strategies open to the Church for dealing with this family of issues. The first would be to interpret canon law and ecclesiology on the basis of papal teachings on "the universal, inviolable, and inalienable" rights which are to be acknowledged by "any human society, if it is to be well-ordered."[52] This view would, if adopted comprehensively, assimilate the Church to the state and other political, economic, and social organizations to the extent that the same human-rights norms would apply. Implementation of such a view would require extensive changes in the church and might well alter the social character of Catholicism in ways which cannot easily be foreseen. In some parts of the world, it may be at odds with the "enculturation" of the local church.

---

[50]The focus of concern here is those members and nonmembers of the Church whose rights are affected by the ministry and the governance of the Church and its institutions. It was also possible for Church officials, when they exercised significant economic and political power, to be involved in violations of human rights, but such violations present no special doctrinal or ecclesiological problem.

[51]The listing of human-rights issues here is drawn from James A. Coriden, "Human Rights in the Church: A Matter of Credibility and Authenticity," in Muller and Greinacher, *The Church and the Rights of Man*, pp. 70-71.

[52]John XXIII, *Pacem in terris*, par. 9. I owe this suggestion to a conversation with James Donlon.

The application of universal norms in the transformation of societies and institutions is a difficult business, even in the best of times. But such an approach, which would amount to restructuring the Church along the lines of an egalitarian universalism, has the attraction of directness and simplicity and would meet the moral demands of many.[53]

A quite different response would be for the Catholic Church to maintain that the principles which rightly apply to human societies in general do not apply to the church because of its divine institution, its supernatural end, its specific objectives and practices, and its dependence on Scripture for its basic norms and structure. This is an approach which would maintain most of the institutional structure and the social style of traditional Catholicism; it would involve a sharp dualism between the norms applying to a participatory, egalitarian, and democratic secular society and the norms applying to a hierarchical and authoritarian religious society.[54] This dualism does not seem to be psychologically untenable, if we look at the historical experience of American Catholicism. It may well be vulnerable to historical arguments to the extent that certain traditional practices and norms have not been universal in the Catholic past and so may be subject to human alteration and development. It also raises questions about how we are to understand the convergence between the development of human society and the fulfillment of humanity in God, a theme which figures prominently in *Gaudium et spes* of Vatican II. For instance, Vatican II affirmed:

> Modern man is on the road to a more thorough development of his own personality, and to a growing discovery and vindication of his own rights. Since it has been entrusted to the Church to reveal the mystery of God, who is the ultimate goal of man, she opens up to man at the same time the meaning of his own existence, that is, the innermost truth about himself.[55]

Are we to suppose that human development proceeds along radically different lines once we enter the ecclesial sphere—and that the innermost truth about humanity is at odds with the development of human personality and human rights?

A variant response which might be offered to support this dualistic view of church and society is to argue that the church is a voluntary association, that its members waive certain rights, and that no injustice is done them when the opportunity to exercise these rights is either denied or not provided. This response involves a highly voluntaristic conception of society and law, which is at variance with the mainstream of Catholic social thought and does not correspond fully to the Church's sense of itself as the "universal sacrament of salva-

---

[53]Egalitarian universalism as a comprehensive norm for nonecclesial societies occupies a central place in *Laborem exercens*.

[54]For a further treatment of this sort of dualism, see John Langan, "Order and Justice under John Paul II," *The Christian Century* 97 (April 30, 1980): 496.

[55]Vatican II, *Gaudium et spes*, par. 41.

tion."[56] But it does have the merit of reminding us of the difference in scale and kind between human-rights issues in the church and the brutal and massive violations of the most basic rights which have occurred in the political life of our times. Also, the voluntaristic view serves to provide the church and its members with the protection of rights which human-rights theory ascribes to all voluntary associations, and it protects the church from judicial and political regulation of a sort which would be burdensome and offensive. The voluntaristic view has more plausibility in justifying the discipline of clerical celibacy and other practices where one can point to an act of consent bearing directly on the practice.

The various issues on the current agenda of the Church which have a human-rights component in them may well have to be treated with different strategies, and their resolution may take quite a long time. It is a sign of the vitality, the relevance, and the ambition of Catholic human-rights doctrine that it leads us to many of the most fundamental and most perplexing social issues of our time. The tension between what a sound human-rights theory seems to demand and what the church does may produce problems of governability within the church and a reaction of incredulity in the face of its teaching. But Catholics can also take courage in the reassuring words of Vatican II:

> Since the Church has a visible and social structure as a sign of her unity in Christ, she can and ought to be enriched by the development of human social life. The reason is not that the constitution given to her by Christ is defective, but that she may understand it more penetratingly, express it better and adjust it more successfully to our time.[57]

The precise shape of the church after it has fully assimilated human-rights theory and the eventual effect on society at large of the Catholic proclamation of human rights and human dignity will be a major part of the history of religion in our time.

---

[56]Ibid., par. 45.
[57]Ibid., par. 44.

4.

JUDAISM AND HUMAN RIGHTS

Daniel F. Polish

The phrase "human rights," itself being of juridic coinage, is of course not employed by classical sources of the Jewish religious tradition. But the system of values and ideas which constitutes the concept "human rights" is hardly absent from the Jewish worldview. On the contrary, those values and ideas are among the beliefs which constitute the very core of Jewish sacred scripture and the tradition of ideas and practices which flows from it. The idea-set which is represented by the phrase "human rights" derives in the Jewish tradition from the basic theological affirmation of Jewish faith. The major holy days commemorate and celebrate various aspects of this idea-set. The history of the Jewish people itself has cast in sharp relief the necessity of those freedoms and protections which the phrase "human rights" connotes.

The narratives of the sacred scriptures of the Jewish people are of a character strikingly different from the myth systems of the peoples of the ancient Near East in whose midst the Jewish people lived and against whose background its sacred texts emerged. That difference reflects a major contrast in values between the Jews and their neighbors and antecedents and underscores a fundamental component of the Jewish *Weltanschauung*. The myths of other ancient peoples consist of histories of the gods, their interactions with one another, and, incidentally, the spawning of humankind and its place in the theocentric cosmos. The monotheism of the Jews' sacred scriptures denotes more than a difference in the number of deities. The text focuses not on the history of that solitary God, but on events in the world which that God created. The Torah begins with the account of the creation of this world. There is not even a clue as to how God was occupied prior to that creation. Indeed, the classical commentators admonish us that it is fruitless to speculate on what happened on the other side of the first letter of the first word of *B'reshit* (Genesis).

The geocentrism—indeed the anthropocentrism—of the Torah underscores a fundamental tenet of Jewish life. The focus of Jewish concern and efforts is not on another world but on this world which we inhabit. This world of ours, then, is to be taken seriously, and our life in it is to be regarded as of the utmost consequence. Beyond that, it is asserted that humankind is to have domain over this world. People do not exist despite the realities of this world, nor does the world persist despite its human inhabitants. Our existence and actions are of the greatest significance. As Ps. 115 notes: "The heavens are the heavens of the

Daniel F. Polish (Jewish) is Rabbi of Temple Israel in Los Angeles. He holds an M.H.L. from Hebrew Union College and a Ph.D. from Harvard University. Until recently the Associate Executive Vice-President of the Synagogue Council of America, he is co-editor (with Eugene Fisher) of *Formation of Social Policy in the Catholic and Jewish Traditions*.

40

Lord, but the earth He hath given to the children of men." This conjunction of the geocentricity of the account of creation and the insistence on human dominion puts concern with human life and the lives of humans at the very center of religious concern.

The recognition of the importance of human life is at the same time both integral to the Jewish faith system and the first and necessary precondition for a belief in human rights. Other elements of that idea-set are similarly central to the worldview of Jewish thought. The notion of human rights flows as a natural extension of the Genesis account of the creation of humanity. The Rabbis, the classical commentators on Torah, were intrigued about why that account is couched in terms of a single individual rather than in terms of multitudes. The story, they state, is cast in this way to teach the value of the worth of the individual. Every individual person is equivalent to that first human created by God. Thus, each person is of supreme value. Whoever harms a single person is as if they had harmed all of God's creation. Whoever benefits a single person is as if they had benefited all creation. Indeed, each of us, equivalent to that first ancestor, is entitled to boast "On account of me was the world created" and, conversely, required to bear on our shoulders the consequences of such responsibility.

The Genesis story enunciates, we are taught, two cardinal principles: the sovereignty of God and the sacredness of the individual.[1] The second motif is underscored by the phrase "in the image of God." Genesis teaches that human beings carry the divine stamp. Each should be treated with the dignity attendant to that station. The *Mekilta*—a Rabbinic commentary on Exodus—suggests that the ten commandments were engraved on parallel tablets of stone, each commandment thus related in some way to its opposite number. In such an arrangement the first commandment—about the absolute sovereignty of God—was juxtaposed to the prohibition of murder. This arrangement, the Rabbis teach, serves to admonish us that to kill a person—to diminish the likeness of God—is tantamount to diminishing the reality of God's own self.

So fundamental to the Jewish worldview is respect for the sanctity of the individual—which grows out of a proper understanding of the Genesis account— that it has even been proposed as the cornerstone of a Jewish value system. Rabbi Akiba, seeking to epitomize the Torah in a single verse, proposed Lev. 19:18, "Love thy neighbor as thyself." But Rabbi Ben Azzai proposed that the broadest value statement in the Torah is from the account of humanity's creation, "This is the record of Adam's line—God in creating humankind, created them in the likeness of God . . ." (Gen. 5:1).[2] The Torah account of the creation of humanity and the tradition of commentary upon it are insistent upon the absolute sanctity of the individual.

Moreover, in discussing the form of the Genesis account of humanity's

---

[1]Samuel Belkin, *In His Image* (New York: Abelard-Schuman, 1960), p. 18.
[2]Sifra, Kedoshim 19:18.

origins, the Rabbis teach that the notion of God's creating an individual person serves to undergird the belief that all people are equal. None of us can claim superiority over another. All of us are *b'nai Adam* (children of Adam)—human, and each equal to that first human. Furthermore, all of us are, in the light of this account, related to one another; all of us are equally descended from the same first ancestor. No one can say that his or her lineage is superior to another's. All of us trace ourselves back to the same roots. In such light, subscription to the Genesis narrative connotes belief in the ultimate importance of every individual and the fundamental equality of all individuals—both essential components of the human-rights idea-set.

If we are to maintain that the Genesis narrative and the tradition which derives from it affirm the equality of all God's children, we must deal with the problem of the treatment accorded to women by Jewish teaching. It has been stated that in myth and law women are treated by Jewish tradition as unequal—indeed as inferior—to men. Some who wish to defend the tradition from such accusations maintain that at every stage of its history the Jewish community was considerably in advance of other societies in the role it accorded women. Others maintain that, far from demeaning women, the status designated to them by Jewish practice had the effect of elevating their position and according them a place of special honor in the polity of Jewish life.

While there may be some truth in such apologetic responses, objectivity demands that we acknowledge that classical Judaism, like all other civilizations from the earliest moments of human consciousness, has, indeed, discriminated against women. While some sectors of Jewish life have sought to redress the inequities inherent in this situation, there remains, in others, a great need to correct the inequalities of status and legal rights still imposed upon Jewish women. Sadly we cannot state that all the injustices have been righted. Instead we must look forward to that time when the issue of the inequality of women is of none but historical interest.

In the meantime, with no desire to suggest that there has not been discrimination against women, it is noteworthy that Jewish religious teaching has in various accounts accorded remarkable theological status to some women. I refer here not to the fact that there have been learned women (Beruria) and even women prophets (Hulda) in our history, nor even that sacred scripture has depicted women as the recipients of revelation. Much more significantly, it was our "mothers," rather than our "fathers," who determined that the covenant itself should be transmitted to the Jewish people. Thus it was Sarah and Rebecca whose actions caused our ancestors, and not those of other peoples, to receive that inheritance. No less remarkably, it was the active exertions of two women—Tamar and Ruth—which established the line that would yield King David and, eventually, the Messiah who would descend from him. Thus, even in the generally bleak picture of the treatment of women in the Jewish tradition, some major exceptions are to be noted.

The not insignificant anomaly of the treatment of women aside, the Jewish tradition has been consistent in advocating the equality of all the children of God. Returning to the classical treatments of the story of Adam, one midrash—Rabbinic elaboration of the biblical text—maintains that to form that first human being God took dirt from all four corners of the world, humus of all shades from which to shape that common ancestor of all people and races. The motif of human equality is sounded again in the story of Noah. With the destruction of all other people, Noah becomes the new Adam, the common ancestor of all who would people the earth. In this account, the commonality underlying racial differentiation is made manifest. The sons of Noah are explicitly identified as the ancestors of the various racial groups. The story indicates an awareness of political distinctions among the various groups of humanity. But there is no escaping the lesson of their ontological equality, for they are clearly sons of one parent: they share the same flesh and blood, the same underlying humanity.

This fundamental equality is rendered in legal terms in the set of mandates given to Noah at the conclusion of the deluge. These rules, which came to be called the Noahide laws, antedate Sinai and are directed equally to all descendants of Noah—all humanity. All who live are regarded as equally defined by this set of "natural" laws. As the laws are equally binding on all people, so they have the effect of identifying all people as equal. Rabbinic law underscores the importance of the Noahide laws as the common laws of all humanity. They become, in effect, the judicial embodiment of the common descent of all humans. All humans are biologically kin by virtue of their common descent from first Adam and then Noah, just as we are cosmically children of the creator God. It is as if the status of the descendants of Noah were cosmicized by Malachi: "Have we not all one Father, hath not one God created us . . .?" The sense of the absolute equality of all people is reflected in a Talmudic account:

> Someone came to Raba and told him: "The general of my town has ordered me to go and kill a named person, and if not, the general will kill me." Raba said to him: "Let the general kill you rather than that you should commit murder. Who knows that your blood is redder? Maybe his blood is redder!"[3]

The commitment to the equality of all people is embodied in the judicial system and process created by the Jewish people. The system of law presented in the Torah and elaborated in Rabbinic legal literature is one that guaranteed a fair trial before an impartial court to all people, homeborn and stranger alike (Lev. 24:22). Judges were forbidden to accept bribes (Deut. 16:19) and were prohibited from showing favoritism in any way—to the needy no less than to the powerful (Lev. 19:15). Throughout the period of their self-determination, the Jewish people prided themselves on the scrupulous fairness of their courts. Equality under law was more than an abstract ideal; it was the concrete embodiment of basic tenets of the theology of the Jewish community.

---

[3]Babylonian Talmud Sanhedrin 74a.

Commitment to the equality of all people may seem, on superficial reflection, to be at odds with another of the theological premises of Israel: the ideal of election. At first glance, election might seem to indicate a privileged place among the family of nations for the Jewish people—a status of manifest inequality. Yet, the major stream of the Jewish tradition itself has not understood election in that light. Election has not been confused with superiority.

According to normative Jewish understanding, God charged the Jews to perform a special task—but did not ascribe to them special merit. Thus Israel could understand God to bless it alongside its historic adversaries: "In that day, Israel shall be a third partner with Egypt and Assyria as a blessing on earth; for the Lord of hosts will bless them, saying, 'Blessed be My people Egypt, My handiwork Assyria, and My very own Israel'" (Is. 19:24-25). More pointedly, Amos addressed the question of election itself and heard God as proclaiming the more universal vision of equality for all humanity: "'Are you not as the children of the Ethiopians to Me, O children of Israel?' says the Lord. 'Have I not brought Israel up out of Egypt? And the Philistines from Caphtor, and the Syrians from Kir?'" (Amos 9:7).

Rabbinic commentaries on the giving of the Torah at Sinai are most revealing on this point. According to one Midrash, God—in desperation at the refusal of all the other nations of the earth to accept the Torah—forced the Jews to acquiesce by holding the mountain over their heads and threatening to bury them under it if they, too, refused. Elsewhere, it is pointed out that, though the Torah was given through the Jews, it was not their exclusive possession. This is the significance of its being given in the wilderness of Sinai. It was not given within the borders of the land of the Jews but in "no-man's land"—that is, in everyone's land. For the Torah was to be the property not of the Jews but of all people. The desert itself symbolized the universality of this Torah which was to be transmitted through the Jewish people. As the sky and sand of the desert belong to all people, so the Torah was the natural property of all people. The concept of election, so understood, in no way contradicts or diminishes the core commitment of Jewish tradition to the fundamental equality of all humankind.

In the face of such a deep-seated belief in human equality, one might expect to find a perfect society with no social inequalities, no political hierarchy, no slavery. Yet even a cursory reading of sacred scriptures reveals that these inequalities did exist in Israel. How shall we respond to the reality of their existence? Perhaps one can find consolation for this situation in the recognition that no society ever attains to the ideal it sets for itself, that peoples should be judged on the goals for which they strive rather than condemned for their failures to achieve them. Or perhaps the Jewish tradition can pride itself on the fact that its prophets attained greatness precisely for speaking out against these inequalities and that the people preserved and honored these negative judgments of itself rather than excising them from its collective memory. But there is more to be said about the questions of slavery and kingship as they existed in the Jewish polity.

While the Torah does recognize the existence of slavery, it can hardly be said to support that practice. The South in the pre-Civil War United States sought to enlist scripture as an advocate for its own "peculiar institution." A fair reading of the Torah reveals, however, that, while it makes account of the existence of this custom of the ancient world, it seems profoundly uncomfortable with it. Indeed, Torah legislation and later Jewish law have the effect of minimizing the evils of slave-holding and progressively limiting the extent of its practice. Jews are proscribed from holding their fellow Jews as slaves, for all are equally servants of the same master. Non-Jewish prisoners of war are permitted to be enslaved; surely this is preferable to their being killed. However, even the slavery of people of other groups is to be understood as a temporary situation rather than a permanent condition. Thus, slaves are to be released after serving a fixed period—six years (Deut. 15:1). There is to be a punishment, not for those who insist on exercising their right to leave at the end of the fixed period of servitude, but for those who demand to remain as slaves (Ex. 21:5-6).

Above all, slaves—while subject to economic disabilities—are not, under Jewish legislation, to be treated as if they had forfeited their personal dignity or their rights. Slaves are to receive humane treatment, and they maintain legal equality. In all, the condition of slaves in ancient Israel was more like that of indentured servants: "No human being can so become the personal property of another as to lose all his individuality."[4]

An extension of the fundamental discomfort with slavery and the insistence upon the basic rights of those who are slaves is the commitment to the rights of all who labor. The Torah and the later Jewish legal tradition are replete with injunctions which protect the rights and well-being of workers. Employers cannot abuse, defraud, or discomfort those who work for them (Deut. 24:14). Employees' comfort is to be promoted and their safety insured. Those who hire out their services and skills to another do not thereby forego the rights inherent in their human status. The limitation of slavery and the mitigation of its evils are in keeping with the reality that the Jewish people itself remembered well its own slave origins and was repeatedly admonished to "remember the heart" of the enslaved.

The same sort of profound ambivalence is evident with respect to the institution of monarchy. Jewish teaching, while recognizing this as the custom of its milieu, seems predisposed against it. The distrust of kings accompanies the first discussion of the subject in scripture (Deut. 17:14-15) as well as the response of the prophet Samuel when the people enjoin him to appoint a king for them (1 Sam. 18:11-18). To prevent kings from abusing their position, Jewish teaching demanded that they be understood to be under the judgment of the same law as their subjects. Kings ruled at the sufferance of God and under the law of God. Kings—like those they ruled—had to obey that law. Thus, they

---

[4]Belkin, *In His Image*, p. 63.

could be called to account for their dereliction of it. The biblical record preserves vivid narratives about kings being chastised for their abuse of position. Nathan denounced David for causing the death of Uriah the Hittite and taking his widow, Bathsheba, as his wife. Elijah pungently excoriated King Ahab and his wife, Jezebel, for having the innocent Naboth killed so that they could expropriate his vineyard. Kings did not exist outside or above the law. They could not abrogate the human rights of those who, like them, were part of the legal system, albeit occupying a different position within that system. The law, to which kings were accountable, guaranteed the rights of the ruled. The Jewish tradition incorporated the prevailing practice of kingship in such a fashion that, rather than contradicting the ideas of equality or the rights of the individual or eroding them in practice, it was made to conform to them, thus underscoring their centrality to the Jewish worldview.

With the end of the monarchy, the Jewish polity reverted to a condition of primitive democracy. Social and economic stratification may have existed, but it had no juridical status. No position or rank was privileged by law. Priests and Levites enjoyed certain prerogatives in the ritual arena, but their position entitled them to no special benefits in the wider sphere and, indeed, subjected them to certain disabilities. When the priestly function was replaced by that of the Rabbi (teacher), it was made explicit that this group was to enjoy no special standing either ritually or legally. Some minor ritual prerogatives were maintained for descendants of the Levites, but in all other matters all Jews were to be strictly equal to one another in ritual as well as legal matters. There was to be no legally enforced hierarchy in Jewish life, a situation which has now prevailed for two millenia.

The core theological affirmations of the Jewish faith demand recognition of the sanctity of the individual and the equality of all individuals as children of God, subject equally to the laws, protection, and love of their Creator. These affirmations, central to Jewish life, serve as the undergirding for the Jewish commitment to the idea-set we call "human rights." From such a commitment flow certain specific affirmations. Specific applications of the ideal of human rights are evidenced throughout Jewish practice. This discussion will show how they are embodied in several of the major holy days of the Jewish calendar.

No manifestation of the ideal of human rights is more fundamental than that of political liberty. That notion stands at the heart of the celebration of *Pesach* (Passover), perhaps the major celebration of the Jewish year and Jewish tradition.[5] This holiday commemorates the central event of biblical—and all Jewish—history, the Exodus from Egypt. In the language of the Haggadah—the liturgical text for that celebration—a proper observance of this holiday carries each celebrant from the degradation of slavery to the exaltation of liberty. Such

---

[5]*Pesach* (Passover) is one of the three major festivals of the year. The other two—*Succot* (Tabernacles) and *Shavuot* (Pentecost)—also commemorate aspects of the Exodus from Egypt.

commemoration cannot but enforce in every Jew the importance of liberty—not for our ancestors alone, but for us, and not for ourselves alone, but for all people.

The central theme of freedom as embodied in the Jewish Exodus is not restricted to that once-a-year celebration of *Pesach* (Passover). It is sounded throughout Jewish observance. The Torah which is read through in its entirety every year, a designated portion being read in the synagogue each week, contains the repeated admonition, "You were slaves in the land of Egypt." The memory of our slave origins and the cost of the loss of freedom is invoked as the warrant for all acts of social righteousness, including the rights of slaves and the necessity for strict equality in juridical procedures which we have already discussed.

The Exodus from Egypt is also understood to be one of the two bases for the celebration of the *Shabbat* (Sabbath)—the weekly day of rest. The other basis is the creation itself—"on the seventh day God rested. . . ." Free people can rest; slaves cannot. Thus, we are enjoined to rest on the seventh day, and not ourselves alone. Even those slaves we have are to be allowed to rest, for, as we have seen, their slavery is not total, only partial and temporary. Their underlying freedom—like ours—is to be commemorated on the day of rest, which is at heart nothing less than a weekly celebration of freedom. The constant repetition of this theme in scripture and in religious observance cannot help but shape an awareness in the Jewish soul of the priceless value of freedom.

Freedom, as taught by the Jewish tradition, is not the exclusive prerogative of majority groups. Jews, as a minority people—from the moment of our inception as a nation, through the period of hegemony in our own land, to this very day—understand the threats to minority rights and value the rights of the minority. One of the most joyful celebrations of the Jewish year is the holiday of *Purim*—the commemoration of the events of the Book of Esther. In that narrative, the Jewish people of Persia, vulnerable because of their minority status, were singled out for destruction by the cunning and powerful Haman. They escaped that plot only narrowly and by extremely fortuitous circumstances. No Jew, hearing that tale, can escape the message that the rights of minorities must be specifically protected and assured, or their minority status can be turned against them to their peril.

If, by some remote chance, one did manage to evade that lesson, it would be propounded in many another forum. The Torah itself demands that the rights of the stranger be as dear as those of the homeborn—for Jews should "know the heart of the stranger, having been strangers in the land of Egypt." Too much of Jewish history is blighted by the tragedies that can befall minorities. No one familiar with the vicissitudes of Jewish history can be callous to the rights of minority peoples.

Jewish tradition is replete with events and practices testifying to the importance of those rights we associate with minorities. The rights of conscience and opinion need not be protected for those in the majority, but those in the minority need to have theirs safeguarded. People are entitled to act in accord-

48

ance with what they believe to be right—even in the face of the law. Thus, the midwives at the beginning of the Book of Exodus defied Pharoah's order to kill all Jewish male infants, so as to do what they believed proper—and they were rewarded for their fidelity to the right. So, too, the martyrs of Jewish history are celebrated for doing what they believed right even in the face of jurisdiction to the contrary. On the afternoon of every *Yom Kippur* (Day of Atonement), Jews read a recounting of those who died "for the sanctification of God's Name" to live a life of fidelity to Torah, even when that was proscribed by the Roman occupiers. Martyrdom for acting on higher values has been considered a positive virtue throughout our history.[6] In these ways Judaism affirms that the right of conscience cannot be abrogated by law—indeed, that one is entitled to violate the law in order to remain true to one's conscientious beliefs.

Not only may one hold what ideas one will:[7] one is also entitled to express those ideas, no matter how unpopular they might be. The prophets of scripture are notable examples of this. No one reading the prophetic books can imagine that the words of the prophets, or the prophets themselves, were popular among the people who heard them; yet, the weight of scriptural precedent is clearly on the side of their importance. Scripture asserts the responsibility of the prophets to deliver their message—their right to utter unpopular ideas. In the Talmud—the *locus classicus* of Jewish law and lore—minority opinions are preserved alongside those of the majority. Rather than recording majority ideas and decisions alone, the Talmud is scrupulous in preserving the words of those whose position did not prevail. The deep respect for dissenting or contrary opinions implicit in this practice stands as a model for the right of people to hold divergent views and to be protected in their right to do so. Minority rights celebrated in the holiday of *Purim* are, in these and other ways, promoted throughout Jewish thought and practice.

One final celebration of a human right is that of the festival of *Chanukah* (The Feast of Lights). This holiday celebrates the specific freedom of religion. When Antiochus Epiphanes sought to demand adherence to one particular state religion, the Jewish populace of Judea under the leadership of Judah Maccabee resisted and prevailed. This winter holiday commemorates not only their valor and victory but also the right of people to liberty in general and, in particular, the right to worship as they please. The sixth chapter of the Book of Daniel, probably composed around the time of the Maccabees, is also concerned with the right of people not to have religious practices either prohibited or imposed upon them by the state.[8]

The importance of the right to freedom of religion is made manifest in

---

[6]For further discussion, see Shalom Spiegel, *The Last Trial* (New York: Pantheon, 1969).

[7]Idolatry, blasphemy, and witchcraft are significant exceptions to this otherwise universal rule.

[8]There is a paradoxical aspect to the story of the Maccabees: It was their descendants, the Hasmoneans, who forced upon a conquered people, the Edomites, mass conversion to

Jewish resistance to those edicts of oppressive rulers which attempted to prohibit Jewish religious practice. Though Jewish liturgy takes special note of such edicts as they were imposed during the period of Roman domination, sadly they were promulgated in many periods of Jewish history: in pagan settings, under Muslim rule, and in Christian Europe into this very century. Our reading of Jewish history is, in part, a celebration of resistance to such efforts to deny Jews the right to practice our tradition or to impose another upon us. Jews rejoice in their perseverance under such inhospitable circumstances and, by so doing, affirm the importance for all people of the right to freedom of religion. Jewish survival itself is testimony to the importance of religious liberty.

The ideals of liberty—the protection of minorities, freedom of conscience and opinion, and freedom of religion—fall within the bounds of what might be called political rights. Recently, another set of rights, more economic in nature, has been propounded—particularly by the nations of the "third world." Is there any warrant for such "economic" rights in the tradition of Jewish thought? There can be little doubt that the Torah and subsequent Jewish teaching argue for the defense of the poor. The Torah is filled with injunctions not to oppress or exploit the poor. Indeed, God "pleads the cause of the poor" (Ps. 146:7), rewarding those who champion the needy, and punishing those who do them wrong (Deut. 24:13). The books of the prophets are replete with denunciations of those who do evil to the poor.[9]

Following from the belief in the rights of the poor, the Jewish community has made active efforts to alleviate their deprivations. Fundamental to such efforts is the idea that God "provides for the needs of all" (Ps. 145:16). If there is scarcity or want, it is not because God has not provided enough but because the systems of distribution are not equitable. Hence, it is incumbent upon humanity to redress that inequity. The laws of the Torah demand that the needs of the poor be attended to. A prime example of this is the legislation which demands that landowners leave portions of their fields and vineyards for the poor so that they do not suffer hunger (Lev. 14:9-10; Deut. 24:19-20). Here, the rights of the needy to live take precedence over property rights. That this injunction was adhered to is witnessed to by the events of the Book of Ruth (2:2 and passim).

Historical and recent Jewish social polity is replete with instances of institutions and practices created for the purpose of feeding the poor, attending to their health needs, and assuring their equal treatment at all the life-cycle moments celebrated by Jewish faith. Among these historic practices of the Jewish community, none has more profound implications than the commitment to education and the insistence that education be made available to people from

---

the Jewish faith. In this they acted contrary to the central theme of the story of their ancestors. Fortunately, this constitutes the only instance of Jews' forcing others to adopt their faith.

[9]Among the most powerful of such statements are Amos 2:6-8, 4:1-3, and 5:8.

every level of society, since in education, in the right to learn a craft, there is hope that the poor can raise themselves out of their condition of deprivation.

Remarkably, Jewish religious literature and Jewish communal practice reflect an attitude that attending to such needs of the poor is an act not of beneficence but of concern, to which the poor are rightfully entitled by virtue of their circumstances. Only through the institution of such practices can the poor gain access to that which God has "provided for . . . all." All this would seem to argue that the idea of "economic rights" does, indeed, have precedent in the teaching and practice of Jewish tradition.

The importance of the ideals of human rights in Judaism is epitomized by the role they play in two central realities of Jewish life—one in the present and one in the future. When, after two millenia of homelessness, a Jewish State was reestablished in our time, it committed itself in its very declaration of independence to embody these values in its polity. Thus, the State of Israel is one of the all-too-few nations of the world in which the law of the land guarantees freedom of conscience, speech, and assembly; safeguards political and judicial freedom; and protects the religious rights of all people. No less significantly, the economic aspect of human rights is manifested in the elaborate and comprehensive system of social services which assures the physical welfare of all citizens of the state. The ideals of human rights are the centerpiece of Israeli law, a testimony to their significance in the Jewish worldview.

The second instance of the embodiment of human rights is in the longed-for future. The importance of the various freedoms which constitute the "political rights" discussed here and of the bounty and health which are the "economic rights" is underscored by the fact that they constitute the Jewish idea of that Messianic time which is the goal of human history—along with the peace which is the complement, or more properly the consequence, of their perfect realization. People long for the time when these ideals will be the normative condition of human life. In cosmic terms, humanity is entitled to them. They are our human rights in the most profound sense. How appropriate, then, that until the arrival of that time of redemption we still-unredeemed humans should labor together to make them our conditions. Rather than simply waiting in hope, we are taught that human efforts should be bent to bring nearer that time when:

> Mercy and truth will meet,
> righteousness and peace embrace.
> Truth will spring up from the earth
> and justice look down from heaven.[10]

---

[10]Ps. 85:11-12.

5.

ON HUMAN RIGHTS AND THE QUR'ANIC PERSPECTIVE

Riffat Hassan

It has been very fashionable for some time to use the term "human rights" rather glibly and to assume that everyone knows what human rights are and from whence they came. It is also commonly assumed that human beings do, in fact, possess human rights. There are two objections to this supposition: one practical, the other philosophical. If most human beings living on this earth today possessed what we call "human rights," we would not be having tens of thousands of persons in virtually every place in the world struggling, either openly or surreptitiously, to secure their "human rights." On the philosophical plane one might argue that "human rights" do exist, even though they are not being exercised by all or even most human beings.

This argument may lead to the question: If human rights exist even though they are not being exercised by all or most human beings (many of whom would be truly astonished to know that they had any such rights), then in what sense do these human rights "exist"? It is a historical fact that human rights have never been, nor are they now, the universal possession of humankind, although it is thirty-three years since the United Nations adopted the International Bill of Human Rights containing the Universal Declaration of Human Rights. It may also be argued that, even though all or most human beings do not exercise their human rights, these human rights remain intact since human beings always can exercise these human rights if and when they choose to do so, because these human rights are universally recognized and enforceable by courts of law. In answer to this argument (having remembered how costly it is to go to a court of law and how right Shakespeare was to bemoan the delays of justice), I cite the words of an eminent Muslim jurist:

> It would be pointless to detail the progressive erosion of human rights in so many contemporary constitutions around the world. Against the rising tide of governmental interference and despotism, they are proving like dykes of straw. Under the guise of creating a "welfare state" or "an egalitarian society", most rights have been deprived of all meaning or significance. In some parts of the world they are directly suspendable and often remain suspended. In states that claim socialist objectives, many of these rights are deprived of enforceability through independent courts; in some constitutions they have been made subject to so many constitutionally authorised inroads as to become devoid of all reality. Even in countries where

Riffat Hassan (Muslim) chairs the Religious Studies Program at the University of Louisville. She received her Ph.D. in Arts from the University of Durham in England. A native of Pakistan, she has published many articles, as well as two books on Iqbal Muhammad; she is currently focusing on the position of women in Islam.

they do not suffer from any of the above limitations, judicial interpretation has, in deference to the idea of State activism and the welfare of the people, severely limited their scope. Perhaps never before has man enjoyed so great a capacity for good and for bad as today; yet never before has an individual felt, as now, so helpless in confrontation with the power and weight of faceless governmental agencies. Power like wealth accrues in the hands of those who wield it. The constitutional limitations of the free world appear to provide little safeguard or guarantee against the continuation of this trend.[1]

When Muslims speak of human rights, they generally speak of a multitude of rights, some of which are derived from a reading of the Qur'an, the Hadith, and the Sunnah, and the rest largely from a study of Islamic history and Islamic law. Most Muslims who speak of human rights also assume that these rights do, in fact, exist and are enforceable by courts of law. A survey of the present-day Muslim world (where each day more and more "human rights" are being eliminated as chastisement for "crimes against God") would hardly provide much evidence to support this assumption. All a Muslim can say today, with any measure of honesty, is that *if* an ideal Islamic society existed, *then* the human rights of those who were part of that society would be recognized and would be enforceable by law.

 In an article on "Islam and Human Rights," A. K. Brohi, another eminent jurist and a Federal Minister in the Pakistan government, made an observation (also made in slightly varying terms by several other Muslim writers writing about Islam and the Western world) which contained a serious allegation and a serious claim. He wrote:

> There is a fundamental difference in the perspectives from which Islam and the West each view the matter of human rights. The Western perspective may by and large be called anthropocentric in the sense that man is regarded as constituting the measure of everything since he is the starting point of all thinking and action. The perspective of Islam on the other hand is theocentric—God-conscious. Here the Absolute is paramount and man exists only to serve his Maker, the Supreme Power and Presence which alone sustains his moral, mental and spiritual make-up, secures the realisation of his aspirations and makes possible his transcendence. . . . [In the West] the rights of man are seen in a setting which has no reference to his relationship to God, but are posited as his inalienable birthright. The student of growth of Western civilization and culture notices throughout that the emphasis is on human rights within an "anthropocentric" perspective of human destiny. Each time the assertion of human rights is made it is done only to secure their recognition from some secular authority such as the state itself or its ruling power. In

---

[1] K. M. Ishaque, "Islamic Law—Its Ideals and Principles," in A. Gauher, ed., *The Challenge of Islam* (London: The Islamic Council of Europe, 1980), p. 157.

marked contrast to this approach the strategy of Islam is to emphasize the supreme importance of our respect for human rights and fundamental freedom as an aspect of the quality of religious consciousness that it claims to foster in the heart, mind and soul of its followers. The perspective is "theocentric" through and through. . . . It seems at first sight, therefore, that there are no human rights or freedoms admissible to man in the sense in which modern man's thought, belief and practice understand them; in essence, the believer has only obligations or duties to God since he is called upon to obey the Divine Law, and such human rights as he is made to acknowledge stem from his primary duty to obey God. Yet paradoxically, in these duties lie all the rights and freedoms. Man acknowledges the rights of his fellow men because this is a duty imposed on him by the religious law to obey God and the Prophet and those who are constituted as authority to conduct the affairs of state. In every thing that a believer does his primary nexus is with His Maker, and it is through Him that he acknowledges his relationship with the rest of his fellowmen as even with the rest of the creation. In the words of the Qur'an, "Man has been created only to serve God!"[2]

It is very characteristic of Muslim apologetics to make statements such as the above. For that reason alone, it is important to point out certain fallacies in what Brohi is saying. First, what he represented as "Western" and described as an "anthropocentric" perspective on human rights is only the perspective of those who either deny the existence of God or regard it as unrelated to human affairs. No one who is properly described as a "Jew" or a "Christian" shares this "anthropocentric" perspective, and—since Jews and Christians form a significant segment of the Western world—it is unwarranted to make such sweeping generalizations regarding the Western perspective. Second, even though many charters of human rights originating in the Western world do not make a direct reference to God, it does not necessarily follow that God-centered or God-related concepts and laws are excluded from them. Reference to God does not necessarily make sacred, nor does nonreference to God necessarily make profane, any human document. To me it seems truly remarkable that an organization such as the United Nations, where every word of every declaration is fought over in an attempt by each country and bloc to protect its vested interest, could arrive at a document such as the Universal Declaration of Human Rights which, though "secular" in terminology, seems to me to be more "religious" in essence than many "*fatwas*" given by Muslim and other religious authorities and agencies. Third, I am not at all sure that the Islamic perspective may correctly be described as "theocentric" in the way in which Brohi appears to be using this term. Certainly, modern Islam's most outstanding thinker, Muhammad Iqbal, who spent his whole life teaching Muslims how to develop their selfhood and who believed that "art, religion and ethics must be judged from the standpoint

[2]A. K. Brohi, "Islam and Human Rights," in Gauhar, *Challenge*, pp. 179-181.

54

of personality,"[3] would have great hesitation in accepting that the highest human morality consisted either in obedience to a law which was externally imposed or in doing one's duty to one's fellow human beings only from a sense of religious constraint. In Iqbal's own words, "There are many who love God and wander in the wilderness, / I will follow the one who loves the persons made by God."[4]

For hundreds of years now, Muslims have been taught that they were created to serve God by obeying those in authority over them and by enduring with patience whatever God willed for them. For hundreds of years, Muslim masses have patiently endured the grinding poverty and oppression imposed on them by those in authority. Not to be enslaved by foreign invaders whose every attempt to subjugate them was met with resistance, Muslim masses were enslaved by Muslims in the name of God and the Prophet, made to believe that they had no rights, only responsibilities; that God was the God of Retribution, not of Love; that Islam was an ethic of suffering, not of joyous living; that they were determined by "*Qismat*," not masters of their own fate. The heroic spirit of Muslim thinkers such as Syed Ahmad Khan and Iqbal, who were born in India in the last century—products not only of a pluralistic society but also of an East-West synthesis—brought about a Renaissance in the Muslim world and liberated Muslims from political bondage. Their work, however, was not completed, since the traditionalism which has eaten away the heart of Islam continues to hold sway over most of the Muslim world. What we are witnessing today in the Muslim world is of extreme interest and importance, for we are living in an age of both revolutions and involutions, of both progression and retrogression, of both great light and great darkness. It is imperative that Muslims rethink their position on all vital issues, since we can no longer afford the luxury of consoling ourselves for our present miseries and misfortunes by an uncritical adulation of a romanticized past. History has brought us to a point where rhetoric will not rescue us from reality and where the discrepancies between Islamic theory and Muslim practice will have to be accounted for.

Although in fact human rights are not universally recognized, universally exercised, or universally enforceable, they are, nonetheless, supremely important; even though many human beings do not understand or enforce them, these are rights which all human beings _ought_ to have. These rights are so deeply rooted in our humanness that their denial or violation is tantamount to a negation or degradation of that which makes us human. These rights came into existence essentially when we did; they were created, as we were, by God in order that our human potential could be actualized. These rights not only provide us with an opportunity to develop all our inner resources, but they also hold before us a vision of what God would like us to be: what God wants us to

___
[3]M. Iqbal, quoted by R. A. Nicholson in the Introduction to *The Secrets of the Self*, translation of *Asrar-e-Khudi* (Farsi) (Lahore: Shaikh Muhammad Ashraf, 1964), p. xxii.
[4]M. Iqbal, *Bang-e-Dara* (Urdu) (Lahore: Shaikh Ghulam Ali and Sons, 1962), p. 151.

strive for and live for and die for. Rights given to us by God are rights which ought to be exercised, since everything that God does is for "a just purpose" (Sura 15:85; 16:3; 44:39; 45:22; 46:3), and renunciation of a God-given right is as virtuous a deed as nonutilization of a God-given talent. Others may or may not recognize our human rights and may or may not facilitate our exercise of these rights, but, as human beings who have a covenantal relationship with God, we must strive under all circumstances to secure and to guard those rights which we believe have been given to us by God and which, therefore, no one else has the right to take away.

Not regarding human rights as a human invention, I do not look for their origin or essence in books of law or history but in those books of scripture which contain God's eternal message and guidance to humankind. By stating, "Towards God is thy limit" (Sura 53:43),[5] the Qur'an—which to me as to other Muslims is the repository par excellence of divine wisdom—gives its readers an infinite worldview embracing every aspect of life. Consequently, it contains references to more "rights" than can be enumerated here. I will, therefore, exercise the prerogative of being selective and mention only those rights which, in my judgment, figure importantly in the Qur'an.

I. General Rights

A. Right to Life

The sanctity and absolute value of human life is upheld by the Qur'an, which states: "Take not life, which God / Hath made sacred, except / By way of justice and law" (Sura 6:151).[6] In Sura 5:35, the Qur'an points out graphically that in essence the life of each individual is comparable to that of an entire community and, therefore, should be treated with great care: "We ordained / For the Children of Israel / That if any one slew / A person—unless it be / For murder or for spreading / Mischief in the land— / It would be as if / He slew the whole people: / And if any one saved a life, / It would be as if he saved / The life of the whole people."

B. Right to Respect

In Sura 17:70, the Qur'an says, "Verily, We have honored every human being." Human beings are deemed worthy of esteem because they are human.

↳ Adam as caliphate

---

[5]Translated by M. Iqbal, *The Reconstruction of Religious Thought in Islam* (Lahore: Shaikh Muhammad Ashraf, 1971), p. 57.

[6]Unless otherwise noted, passages from the Qur'an cited here in verse form are taken from A. Y. Ali, *The Holy Qur'an* (Smithtown, NY: McGregor and Werner, Inc., 1946). Those in prose are taken from G. A. Parwez, *Islam: A Challenge to Religion* (Lahore: Idara-e-Tulu'-e-Islam, 1968).

56

Being human means, according to the Qur'anic perspective, that human beings alone of all creation chose to accept the "trust" of freedom of the will (Sura 33:72). Human beings can exercise freedom of the will because they possess the rational faculty, which is what distinguishes them from all other creatures (Sura 2:30-34). Because human beings are made "in the best of moulds," though they can abase themselves to be "the lowest of the low" (Sura 95:4-6), and can think, and can have knowledge of right and wrong, and are able to strive to do the good and avoid the evil, they have the potential to be God's vicegerents on earth. On account of the promise that is contained in being human, the humanness of all human beings is to be respected and regarded—to use a Kantian expression—as an end in itself.

C. Right to Justice

In the Qur'an, tremendous emphasis is put on the right to seek justice and the duty to do justice: "O ye who believe! be steadfast witnesses for Allah in equity; and not let enmity of any people seduce you that ye deal not justly. Deal justly, that is nearer to your duty. Observe your duty to Allah" (Sura 5:9). Likewise, "O ye who believe! Be ye staunch in justice; witnesses for Allah, even though it be against your own selves, or your parents, or your kindred, whether (the case be of) a rich man or a poor man, for Allah is nearer unto both (than ye are). So follow not passion lest ye lapse (from truth), nor ye distort truth or turn aside; verily God is well informed of what ye do" (Sura 4:135).

In the context of justice, the Qur'an uses two concepts: "'adl" and "ihsan." Both are enjoined (Sura 16:91), and both are related to the idea of "balance," but they are not identical in meaning. A. A. A. Fyzee, a well-known scholar of Islamic law, defined "'adl" as "to be equal, neither more nor less," and wrote, "in a Court of Justice the claims of the two parties must be considered evenly, without undue stress being laid upon one side or the other. Justice introduces the balance in the form of scales that are evenly balanced."[7] Abu'l Kalam Azad, a famous translator of the Qur'an and a noted writer, described "'adl" in similar terms: "What is justice but the avoiding of excess. There should be neither too much nor too little; hence the use of scales as the emblems of justice."[8] Lest anyone try to do too much or too little, the Qur'an states that no human being can carry another's burden (Sura 53:38) or have anything without striving for it (Sura 53:39).

It is important to note here that, according to the Qur'anic perspective, justice is not to be interpreted as absolute equality of treatment, since human beings are not equal as far as their human potential or their human situation is concerned. Thus, while upholding the principle that the humanness of all human beings is to be respected, the Qur'an maintains that the recognition of individual

---

[7]A. A. A. Fyzee, *A Modern Approach to Islam* (Lahore: Universal Books, 1978), p. 17.
[8]Ibid.

"merit" is also a fundamental human right. The Qur'an teaches that merit is not determined by lineage or sex or wealth or worldly success or religion–but by "righteousness." Righteousness consists not only of "just belief" ("*iman*") but also of "just action" ("*'amal*") as pointed out with clarity in Sura 2:177: "It is not righteousness / That ye turn your faces / Towards East or West; / But it is righteousness– / To believe in God / And the Last Day, / And the Angels, / And the Book, / And the Messengers; / To spend of your substance, / Out of love for Him, / For your kin, / For orphans, / For the needy, / For the wayfarer, / For those who ask, / And for the ransoms of slaves; / To be steadfast in prayer, / And practice regular charity; / To fulfill the contracts / Which ye have made; / And to be firm and patient, / In pain (or suffering) / And adversity, / And throughout / All periods of panic. / Such are the people / Of truth, the God-fearing." Sura 49:13 tells us that "the most honored of you in the sight of God is the most righteous of you," and Sura 4:95 says: "Not equal are those / Believers who sit (at home) / And receive no hurt, / And those who strive / And fight in the cause / Of God with their goods / And their persons. / God hath granted / A grade higher to those / Who strive and fight / With their goods and persons / Than to those who sit (at home). / Unto all (in Faith) / Hath God promised good: / But those who strive and fight / Hath He distinguished / Above those who sit (at home) / By a special reward."

Just as it is in the spirit of "*'adl*" that special merit be considered in the matter of rewards, so also special circumstances must be considered in the matter of punishments(In the case of punishment for crimes of "unchastity," for instance, the Qur'an, being non-sexist, prescribes identical punishments for a man or a woman who is proved guilty (Sura 2:2), but it differentiates between different classes of women; for the same crime, a slave woman would receive half, and the Prophet's consort double, the punishment given to a "free" Muslim woman (Sura 4:25; 33:30). Making such a distinction shows compassion for the morally "disadvantaged," while upholding high moral standards for others, particularly those whose actions have a normative significance.)

While constantly enjoining "*'adl*," the Qur'an goes beyond this concept to "*ihsan*," literally "restoring the balance by making up a loss or deficiency."[9] In order to understand this concept, it is necessary to understand the nature of the ideal community or society ("*ummah*") envisaged by the Qur'an. The word "*ummah*" comes from the root "*umm*," or "mother." The symbols of a mother and motherly love and compassion are also linked with the two attributes most characteristic of God, namely "*Rahman*" and "*Rahim*," both of which are derived from the root "*rahm*," meaning "womb." The ideal "*ummah*" cares about all of its members as an ideal mother cares about all of her children, knowing that all are not equal and that each has different needs. While encouraging any one of her children to be parasitical would be injurious and unjust, not

[9]G. A. Parwez, *Tabweeb-ul-Qur'an* (Urdu) (Lahore: Idara-e-Tulu'-e-Islam, 1977), vol. 1, p. 78.

only to her other children but also to the one who betrays its human promise and lives—in Iqbal's terminology—by "begging," she feels that she has the right to make up the deficiency of a child who, despite its best efforts, still cannot meet the requirements of life. "*Ihsan*" is that which secures what even "*'adl*" cannot; it shows the Qur'an's sympathy for the downtrodden, oppressed, or weak classes of human beings (such as women, slaves, orphans, the poor and infirm, and minorities).

D. Right to Freedom

There is much in the Qur'an to suggest that it would support Jean Jacques Rousseau's famous statement, "Man is born free, and everywhere he is in chains." A large part of the Qur'an's concern is to free human beings from the chains which bind them: traditionalism, authoritarianism (religious, political, economic), tribalism, racism, sexism, and slavery.

It is obvious that God alone is completely free and not subject to any constraint. The human condition necessitates that limits be set to what human beings may or may not do, so that liberty does not degenerate into license. Recognizing the human propensity toward dictatorship and despotism, the Qur'an says with startling clarity and emphasis: "It is not right for man that God should give him the Book of Law, power to judge and (even) Prophethood, and he should say to his fellow-beings to obey his orders rather than those of God. He should rather say: Be ye faithful servants of God by virtue of your constant teaching of the Book and your constant study of it" (Sura 3:79).

The institution of human slavery is, of course, extremely important in the context of human freedom. Slavery was widely prevalent in Arabia at the time of the advent of Islam, and the Arab economy was based on it. The insistence in the Qur'an that slaves be treated in a just and humane way[10] (e.g., Sura 4:36) is generally recognized, as is the effort made by the Qur'an toward the emancipation of slaves (Sura 24:33; 4:92; 5:89; 9:60; 58:3; 2:177). But a number of writers, including well-known Muslim writers such as Abu'l Ala Maududi[11] and Muhammad Qutb,[12] are of the opinion that, though early Islam did much to alleviate the suffering and uplift the status of slaves, slavery was not abolished by the Qur'an. G. A. Parwez, who has spent over fifty years in Qur'anic scholarship, does not agree with this opinion (which, unfortunately, would appear to be the majority opinion) and says:

> In every conceivable way, the Qur'an discouraged slavery and im-
> proved the lot of the slaves. The Muslims were urged to be kind and

---

[10]R. Roberts, *The Social Laws of the Qur'an* (Lahore: Sang-e-Meel Publications, 1978), p. 56.

[11]See, e.g., A. A. Maududi, *Human Rights in Islam* (Lahore: Islamic Publications, 1977), pp. 18-19.

[12]See, e.g., M. Qutb, *Islam: The Misunderstood Religion* (Lahore: Islamic Publications, 1972), pp. 24-52.

considerate to their slaves. They were told that to emancipate a slave was a meritorious act. They could atone for some of their offences by setting a slave free. Thus the number of slaves was gradually reduced and society was made less dependent on slave labor. The words "whom your right hand possessed" occurring in the Qur'an are in the past tense and refer to those who had already been enslaved. When they were emancipated through a gradual process, slavery died a natural death. The main source of slaves—men and women—was prisoners in war. The Qur'an laid down that they should be set free either for a ransom or as a favor (Sura 47:4). The door for future slavery was thus closed by the Qur'an forever. Whatever happened in subsequent history was the responsibility of the Muslims and not of the Qur'an.[13]

Keeping in mind the great emphasis which the Qur'an places on human dignity and human freedom, it seems to me inconceivable that any other reading of Sura 47:4 is possible. That so few Muslims have accepted the idea that slavery was, indeed, abolished by the Qur'an indicates how reluctant the others have been to let go of the worst possible kind of power-obsession: to seek to own another human being made by God. It is interesting to reflect on the method and morality of how the majority of Muslims have understood the spirit of Qur'anic ethics. On the basis of two statements related to the drinking of alcohol—"They ask thee / Concerning wine and gambling. Say: 'In them is great sin, / And some profit, for men; / But the sin is greater / Than the profit'" (Sura 2:219); and "O ye who believe! / Intoxicants and gambling, / (Dedication of) stones, / And (divination by) arrows, / Are an abomination— / Eschew such (abomination), / That ye may prosper"—the Muslims have universally concluded that the drinking of alcohol is absolutely prohibited by the Qur'an. On the basis of a much larger and no less emphatic statement reflecting a deep concern with the problem of slavery, Muslims have not similarly concluded that slavery was prohibited by the Qur'an. Because the Qur'an does not state explicitly that slavery is abolished, it does not follow that it is to be continued, particularly in view of the numerous ways in which the Qur'an seeks to eliminate this absolute evil. A Book which does not give a king or a prophet the right to command absolute obedience from another human being could not possibly sanction slavery in any sense of the word, but this argument does not appeal to those Muslims who hypocritically follow the letter and not the spirit of the law of God.

The greatest guarantee of personal freedom for a Muslim lies in the Qur'anic decree that no one other than God can limit human freedom (Sura 42:21) and in the statement that "Judgment is only Allah's" (Sura 12:40).[14] As pointed out by K. M. Ishaque,

[13]Parwez, *Islam*, p. 346.
[14]Translated by K. A. Hakim, *Fundamental Human Rights* (Lahore: Institute of Islamic Culture, 1975), p. 15.

60

> The Qur'an gives to responsible dissent the status of a fundamental
> right. In exercise of their powers, therefore, neither the legislature
> nor the executive can demand unquestioning obedience. . . . The
> Prophet, even though he was the recipient of Divine revelation, was
> required to consult the Muslims in public affairs. Allah addressing
> the Prophet says: ". . . and consult with them upon the conduct of
> affairs. And . . . when thou art resolved, then put thy trust in Allah"
> (Sura 3:159).[15]

Since the principle of mutual consultation (*"shura"*) is mandatory (Sura 42:38),
it is a Muslim's fundamental right to participate in as many aspects of the
community's life as possible.

Muslims generally agree that the Qur'anic proclamation in Sura 2:256 ("Let
there be no compulsion / In religion: Truth stands out / Clear from Error: whoever / Rejects Evil and believes / In God hath grasped / The most trustworthy /
Hand-hold, that never breaks") means that non-Muslims are not be coerced into
professing Islam and that it is the human right of non-Muslims living in territories governed by Muslims that they should have the freedom to follow their
own faith-traditions without fear or harassment. But the impulse to proselytize
has always been strong in Muslims—as in Christians—even though a number of
Qur'anic passages state quite clearly that the mission of the Prophet (and the
Muslims) to non-Muslims consists only of a faithful transmission of the message
of God and that the Prophet (and the Muslims) ought not to feel responsible for
the religious or moral choices made by other Muslims or by non-Muslims after
they have received the message of God. For instance, "If it had been God's Plan
/ They would not have taken / False gods: but We / Made thee not one / To
watch over their doings, / Nor art thou set / Over them to dispose / Of their
affairs" (Sura 6:107).[16] The Qur'an, regarding its own truth as clear and self-
evident, does not require the zeal of Muslims to prove it.

It is interesting and important to observe that professing Islam does not, in
and by itself, give a Muslim any kind of advantage over any other believer:
"Those who believe (in the Qur'an), / And those who follow the Jewish (scriptures), / And the Christians and the Sabians, / Any who believe in God / And the
Last Day, / And work righteousness, / Shall have their reward / With their Lord"
(Sura 2:62). On the basis of this verse, all who believe in God and the hereafter
and work righteousness can claim not only religious freedom but also religious
equality. However, many Muslims—disregarding this and similar verses and the
Qur'anic statement that God is *"rabb-a-'alamin,"* God of all peoples, whose
mercy extends to all creatures (Sura 7:156)—would vigorously dispute the right
of non-Muslims to claim religious equality with them. Iqbal was an exceptional
Muslim, in that he could go so far as to say: "The infidel with a wakeful heart

---

[15]Ishaque, "Islamic Law," pp. 167-169.
[16]See also Sura 10:99; 16:82; 18:29; 42:48.

praying to an idol is better than a Muslim who is sleeping in the mosque."[17]

The Qur'an recognizes the human right of religious freedom, not only in the case of other believers in God, but also in the case of pagans (if they are not aggressing upon the Muslims). For instance: "If one amongst the Pagans / Ask thee for asylum, / Grant it to him, / So that he may hear the word / Of God; and then escort him / To where he can be secure" (Sura 9:6); and "Revile not ye / Those whom they call upon / Besides God, lest / They out of spite / Revile God / In their ignorance. / Thus have We made / Alluring to each people / Its own doings. / In the end will they / Return to their Lord, / And We shall then / Tell them the truth / Of all that they did" (Sura 6:108).

In the context of the human right to religious freedom, it is necessary to mention that, according to traditional Islam, the punishment for apostasy is death. In other words, a person who is born a Muslim or who becomes a Muslim is to be put to death if he or she later chooses to renounce Islam. There is nothing in the Qur'an which suggests any punishment at all, let alone the punishment of death, for a Muslim who renounces Islam. There is absolutely no reason to assume that the Qur'anic dictum, "Let there be no compulsion in religion" (Sura 2:256), which modern Muslims apply with such magnanimity to non-Muslims does not or should not apply to Muslims also. (I believe that the death penalty was not meant to be a punishment for apostasy alone but for apostasy accompanied by "acts of war" against the Muslims. Muslim legists, however, obliterated the distinction between the exercise of a human right and the violation of others' human rights in order to terrify the "wavering" Muslims into remaining in the fold of Islam.)

The right to freedom includes the right to be free to tell the truth, without which a just society cannot be established. The Qur'anic term for truth is "*Haqq*," also one of God's most important attributes. Standing up for the truth is a right and a responsibility which a Muslim may not disclaim even in the face of the greatest danger or difficulty (Sura 4:135). While the Qur'an commands believers to testify to the truth, it also instructs the society not to harm the person so testifying (Sura 2:282).[18]

E. Right to Privacy

The Qur'an recognizes the need for privacy as a human right and lays down rules for how the individual's life in the home may be protected from undue intrusion from within or without (Sura 24:27-28; 33:53; 24:58; 49:12).

---

[17]M. Iqbal, *Javid Nama* (Farsi) (Lahore: Shaikh Mubarak Ali, 1947), p. 40.
[18]G. A. Parwez, "Bunyadi Haquq-e-Insaniqat (Fundamental Human Rights)" (Urdu), *Tulu'-e-Islam* (Lahore), November, 1981, pp. 34-35.

F. Right to Protection from Slander, Backbiting, and Ridicule

The Qur'an acknowledges the right of human beings to be protected from defamation, sarcasm, offensive nicknames, and backbiting (Sura 49:11-12). It also points out that no person is to be maligned on grounds of assumed guilt and that those who engage in malicious scandal-mongering will be grievously punished in both this world and the next (Sura 24:16-19). The Qur'an also protects the right of a human being to be treated with sensitivity and compassion. It states with solemn simplicity: "God loves not that evil / Should be noised abroad / In public speech, except / Where injustice hath been / Done; for God / Is He who heareth / And knoweth all things. / Whether ye publish / A good deed or conceal it / Or cover evil with pardon, / Verily God doth blot out / (Sins) and hath power / (In the judgment of values)" (Sura 4:148-149).

G. Right to "The Good Life"

The Qur'an upholds the right of the human being not only to life but to "the good life." This good life, made up of many elements, becomes possible when a human being is living in a just environment. According to Qur'anic teaching, justice is a prerequisite for peace, and peace is a prerequisite for human development. In a just society the human rights mentioned earlier may be exercised without difficulty.

H. Other Rights.

In addition to those rights, there are several others which are important and should be mentioned in passing: (1) the right to a secure place of residence (Sura 2:85); (2) the right to a means of living (Sura 11:6; 6:156); (3) the right to protection of one's personal possessions (Sura 2:29); (4) the right to seek knowledge (which is emphasized perhaps more than any other right by the Qur'an); (5) the right to develop one's aesthetic sensibilities and enjoy the bounties created by God (Sura 7:32); (6) the right to protection of one's covenants (Sura 17:34; 5:1; 3:177); (7) the right to move freely (Sura 67:15); (8) the right to seek asylum if one is living under oppression (Sura 4:97-100); (9) the right to social and judicial autonomy for minorities (Sura 5:42-48); and (10) the right to protection of one's holy places (Sura 9:17) and the right to return to one's "spiritual center." (According to the Qur'anic teaching—Sura 3:96; 5:97; 22:25—the *Ka'ba* is the spiritual center of all humankind. However, the government of Saudi Arabia does not permit any non-Muslim to enter Mecca or to perform the pilgrimage which was proclaimed to all humankind by Abraham, as pointed out by Sura 3:96; 22:26; 2:125.)

II. Rights of Man, Woman, and Child

According to the Qur'an, God created man and woman from a single life-cell or spirit (Sura 4:1; 7:189; 16:72; 30:21). Both man and woman have male and female components (Sura 49:13), and both—together—constitute the human species. It is a clear teaching of the Qur'an that man and woman are equal in the sight of God (Sura 3:195; 4:124; 9:71-72; 16:97; 33:35; 40:40). Being equal before God who is the ultimate source of life and the ultimate standard of value, man and woman cannot become unequal to each other in essence. In fact, however, they are extremely unequal in almost all Muslim societies, where the superiority of man over woman is taken to be self-evident. Having spent seven years in study of the Qur'anic passages relating to women, I am convinced that the Qur'an is not biased against women and does not discriminate against them. On the contrary, because of its protective attitude toward all downtrodden and oppressed classes, it appears to be weighted in many ways in favor of women. But the interpretations of the Qur'an by men (women to this day have never had the right to interpret the Qur'an) have distorted the truth almost beyond recognition and have made the Qur'an a means of keeping women in bondage, physically and spiritually. Many Muslims, when they speak of human rights, either do not speak of women's rights at all[19] or are mainly concerned with the question of how a woman's chastity may be protected.[20] (They are apparently not very worried about men's "chastity.") The most gross violation of human rights in Muslim societies is that of the rights of women, who for centuries have been deprived of the right to be fully human. Muslims say with great pride that Islam abolished female infanticide; true, but it must also be mentioned that one of the most common crimes in many Muslim countries (e.g., Pakistan) is the murder of a woman by her husband. These so-called "honor-killings" are actually extremely dishonorable and are frequently used to camouflage other kinds of crimes.

Female children are discriminated against from the moment of birth, for it is customary in Muslim societies to celebrate the birth of a son and to bemoan the birth of a daughter. Many, if not most, girls are married when they are still minors, even though marriage in Islam is a contract and presupposes that the contracting parties are both consenting adults. Even though so much Qur'anic legislation is aimed at protecting the rights of women in the context of marriage (e.g., Sura 4:19; 24:33; 2:187; 9:71; 7:189; 30:21; 4:4), women can never claim equality with their husbands. The husband, in fact, is regarded as his wife's gateway to heaven or hell and the arbiter of her final destiny. That such an idea can exist within the framework of Islam—which totally rejects the idea of redemption, of any intermediary between a believer and the Creator—represents both a profound irony and a great tragedy.

---

[19]E.g., R. A. Jullundrhi, "Human Rights in Islam," in A. D. Falconer, ed., *Understanding Human Rights* (Dublin: Irish School of Ecumenics, 1980).

[20]E.g., Maududi, *Human Rights*.

64

Although the Qur'an presents the idea of what we today call a "no-fault divorce" and does not make any adverse judgments about divorce (e.g., Sura 2:231; 2:241), Muslim societies have made divorce for women extremely difficult, both legally and through social penalties. Although the Qur'an states clearly that the divorced parents of a minor child must decide by mutual consultation how the child is to be raised and that they must not use the child to hurt or exploit each other (Sura 2:233), in most Muslim societies women are deprived of both their sons (generally at age seven) and their daughters (generally at age twelve), thus being subjected to unutterable cruelty. Although polygamy was intended by the Qur'an to be for the protection of orphans and widows (Sura 4:2-3), in practice Muslims have made it a dreadful and dehumanizing instrument for the brutalizing of women's sensibilities. Although the Qur'an made it possible for women to receive not only an inheritance upon the death of a close relative but also other bequests or gifts during the lifetime of a benevolent caretaker, Muslim societies have disapproved greatly of the idea of giving wealth to a woman in preference to a man, even when her need or circumstances warrant it. Although the purpose of the Qur'anic legislation dealing with women's dress and conduct (Sura 24:30-31; 33:59) was to make it safe for women to go about their daily business (since they have the right to earn money, as witnessed by Sura 4:32) without fear of sexual harassment, Muslim societies have put many of them behind veils and locked doors on the pretext of protecting their chastity, forgetting that according to the Qur'an (Sura 4:15) confinement to their homes was not the normal way of life for chaste women but a punishment for "unchastity."

A few words need to be said about the human rights of (minor) children according to Qur'anic teaching. Children have a right to life (Sura 81:8-9; 16:57-59; 17:31); a right to proper nurture and education (Sura 17:31; 2:233); a right to be maintained financially by the father or his heir(s) (Sura 24:61), but to be brought up according to the wishes of both parents (Sura 2:233); and a right to have their interests protected by the Islamic society in which they live, should they become orphaned (Sura 4:2-3 and numerous other references). Anyone reading the Qur'an is deeply touched by its concern for the welfare of orphans and particularly by its reminder to the Prophet, "And He found thee / In need, and made / Thee independent / Therefore treat not / The orphan with harshness, / Nor repulse the petitioner / (Unheard); / But the Bounty / Of thy Lord— / Rehearse and proclaim" (Sura 93:8-11).

III. In the End

In my judgment, the Qur'an is a very liberating document which holds before us a sublime vision of our human potential, our destiny, and our relationship with God and God's creatures. If Muslims were to exercise all the human rights granted to humankind by God, they would create a Paradise on earth and have no need to spend their time and energy dreaming about the *"hur"* promised in the afterlife. Unfortunately, at this time the spectrum before us appears very bleak, as more and more human rights disappear under the pressure of mounting fanaticism and traditionalism in many areas of the Muslim world. I am particularly concerned about serious violations of human rights pertaining to the rights of women, the rights of minorities, the right of the accused to due process of law, and the right of the Muslim masses to be free of dictatorships. In the end we have what seems to be an irreconcilable gulf between Qur'anic ideals and the realities of Muslim living. Can this gulf be bridged? To me, the answer is immaterial, because those of us who believe that human rights cannot be abandoned, even when they are being denied and aborted, will continue to strive and hope and pray for the securing of these rights—regardless of the chances of success or failure.

6.

THE BUDDHIST PERSPECTIVE ON HUMAN RIGHTS

Kenneth K. Inada

In one respect the world is becoming smaller and smaller, but in another it is becoming larger and larger. The components of the world have changed and shifted so much that we can look at the world in terms of either its constricted or its expanded nature. Take, for example, the rise of new nations. This numerical increase, which we did not anticipate forty years ago, has given us an expanded outlook of the world. However, all the nations share common interests, especially with respect to the welfare of their respective citizens, and, as nations focus on common issues, the world at large can be seen as narrowed down or constricted. Yet, the truth of the matter is that, in dealing with issues, it is natural to view the world in its dipolar nature, with both the narrow special focus and the focus on the broadened nature of things, for the "narrow view" gives us a focus or concentration on an issue, and the "broader view" gives us the extension of the issue or its wider application.

The International Bill of Human Rights, promulgated by the United Nations General Assembly on December 10, 1948, is a case in point.[1] Although the question of human rights is a concern for each nation, it must at the same time apply to all nations. To have some nations upholding the rights while some others do not is a flagrant contradiction of the Bill, for to have universal acceptance means at once to have universal cogency. The two cannot be separated or isolated; there should be no exceptions. Yet, as we have witnessed in the last thirty years or so, the dual nature of universal acceptance and cogency has been made a mockery. The dipolar nature exists generally on the level of perfunctory function. There are always stumbling blocks to viewing issues individually as well as within the context of a broadened application. An imbalance, a disparity, results in the nature of individual existence and its place and role in the larger social and political context. This situation exists within nations as well as on the international level.

In many respects we have arrived at an impasse in human relations. How did this come about? Could it be that the dichotomy between human and national relations has widened? Could it be that the focus has shifted drastically in favor of national relations rather than human relations? What brought about this peculiar situation? Can we, finally, stem the tide of this ever-widening gap which

---

[1]See pp. 105-109, below.

Kenneth K. Inada (Buddhist) is a Professor of Philosophy at the State University of New York at Buffalo. He holds an M.A. from the University of Chicago and a Ph.D. from the University of Tokyo. He is the managing editor of the *Journal of Buddhist Philosophy* and author of the forthcoming *The Buddhist Way*.

now exists in the United Nations and which perpetuates the divisive forces within it? These are hard questions we face, but ones to which we must properly address ourselves in pushing forward to some understanding and accommodation of the crucial question on human rights.

It should be emphasized at the outset that the nature of human rights is not an abstraction, although we are inclined to treat it so. It points at concrete everyday occurrences. Yet it cannot be denied that its nature is usually glossed over or neglected in human intercourse, due to the overwhelming external forces that impinge on everyone—as seen, for example, in acts of political expediencies. It thus loses much of its meaning and force and becomes an abstract quantity by default, although this is clearly counter to the good faith and intention placed on it initially. Because of the external forces, even in an allegedly democratic nation such as the United States, we experience either pockets of human rights in operation or their shadowy abstraction ensconced in the written documents whose interpretation or translation into meaningful acts is usually beyond the understanding of ordinary citizens.

We are, perhaps, living in one of the saddest moments in that, despite the ever-maturing process of the world—the developmental movement of the world taken in its totality—the estrangement of persons in society has increased and even become a fact of life. Where scientism and its attendant materialism, heavily spiced with self-interest and gain, have taken hold of the world, persons have become silent but unequal partners in "world progress." The gulfs are many and varied, but the one which is most ominous and poignant is undoubtedly the inequalities in human rights. The present may thus be an opportune time to reassess the situation and to bring into play the collective wisdom of the world, East and West.

From the Eastern sector, the Buddhist position is unique. While it claims no panacea for the many-faceted human ills of the world, its views on the matter, propounded over 2,500 years ago, are still relevant and cogent today. I will explore its implications.

In the last 100 years, Buddhists have been able to rally around their faith twice in terms of the promulgation of Buddhist principles. While the promulgation was taken seriously each time by the Buddhists, the impact on the West was negligible, even though in both instances the leaders were Westerners, one American and one British.

The first was written by Colonel Henry Steele Olcott in 1891, as a show of force of all Buddhists during the height of Asian colonization. Olcott was an American who had served in the Civil War and subsequently joined the theosophical movement, eventually co-founding the Theosophical Society of New York in 1875 with Madame H. P. Blavatsky. This eventually took him to India and Ceylon. It was in Ceylon (now Sri Lanka) that he was impressed by the profound Buddhist way of life, and he officially embraced it in 1880. At the same time, he saw that Buddhism was neglected by the general populace and that it remained in a deplorable state. How could such a noble way of life be in such sad straits and circumstances? He spent the rest of his life uplifting the Buddhist lot and was soon recognized as the single most influential force in the revival of Buddhism in all its aspects—religious, educational, and cultural. In the process, he offered to the world the "Fourteen Fundamental Buddhistic Beliefs."[2] For a relatively recent initiate to Buddhism, Olcott had quite a good grasp of its essentials. He lived the life of a Buddhist and saw its successful revival before his death. However, Asia and Buddhism remained largely unknown in Western eyes up to World War II.

It was immediately at the end of hostilities of World War II that the long-time editor and founder of *The Middle Way* magazine in London, lawyer Christmas Humphreys, seized the opportunity and occasion to rally the Buddhist world together, just as Colonel Olcott had done some fifty years earlier. Humphreys worked as a trial lawyer in the Tokyo War Crimes Trial, during which time he formulated the "Twelve Principles of Buddhism."[3] As with Olcott's document, Humphreys' was widely circulated and sanctioned by leaders of both the Theravāda and Mahāyāna traditions.

Olcott's Fourteen Beliefs and Humphreys' Twelve Principles generally coincide on the essentials or cover the same ground. They reveal the fundamental nature of Buddhism succinctly. The essentials are culled from the Buddhist canons, but it seems almost as if they speak directly to the question of human rights, as well as animal rights. For example, Olcott's first belief asserts: "Buddhists are taught to show the same tolerance, forbearance, and brotherly love to all men, without distinction; and an unswerving kindness towards the members of the animal kingdom."[4] The casual reader of that statement might not be easily convinced of Buddhist motives and might look upon it as a platitude, for such terms as "tolerance," "forbearance," "brotherly love," and "kindness" are common to all religions of the world. There is nothing new about them. The Buddhist assertion, however, takes on a deeper meaning when the essential doctrines are brought into play. So, the fifth belief states: "Śākyamuni [the Buddha] taught that ignorance produces desire, unsatisfied desire is the cause of rebirth, and rebirth the cause of sorrow. To get rid of sorrow, therefore, it is necessary to escape from rebirth; it is necessary to extinguish desire; and to extinguish desire, it is necessary to destroy ignorance."[5]

The key ideas here are ignorance, desire, rebirth, and sorrow, seemingly common terms. Taken separately, and in their translation, they are simple enough to understand. However, given in the manner presented, where one leads to another and then back again, it becomes rather difficult to comprehend their

---

[2]"The Fourteen Fundamental Buddhistic Beliefs" is found in the essay by Buddhadasa P. Kirthisinghe, "Colonel Henry Steele Olcott, The Great American Buddhist," in his *Colonel Olcott: His Service to Buddhism*. The Wheel Publication 281. (Kandy, Sri Lanka: Buddhist Publication Society, 1981), pp. 14-17.

[3]"The Twelve Principles of Buddhism" is in the Appendix of Christmas Humphreys, *A Buddhist Students' Manual* (London: Buddhist Lodge Publication, 1951), pp. 275-279.

[4]Kirthisinghe, "The Great American Buddhist," p. 14.

[5]Ibid., p. 15.

full implications, because the translated terms have a deeper, if not novel, meaning in the original language.

For example, "ignorance" refers to the Pali *avijjā*, which depicts more than rational ignorance, as it refers to the total state of existential unclarity, that is, not being able to understand the full nature of one's existence within the total context. After all, the rational realm is not the whole of existence. It goes along with or is complemented by elements other than the rational or what may be referred to generally as the "nonrational" realm.

"Desire" refers to *tanhā*, which is more than the ordinary desiring function, for it designates the insatiable and overwhelmingly unchecked force of carving out one's own being. In this respect, everything is strained or forced, and thus the element of attachment or clinging becomes a fact.

"Rebirth" is the translation of *patisandhi*, which depicts the microscopic re-linking phenomena of momentary existence characterized by the "Wheel of Life." In Buddhism, the concept of impermanence is basic to life. When the historical Buddha was enlightened, he captured the supreme moment of existence, but at the same time he realized that the basis for universal suffering in the world is attributed to the failure to understand the impermanent or momentary nature of the life-process. Thus, rebirth is a convenient but unique term used to describe how the existential process goes on in virtue of the attachment to the empirical nature of being.

Finally, "sorrow" is the translation of *dukkha*, which is more than mere commiseration in psychological or emotional terms, for it refers to the universal nature of the human condition which covers the total psychophysical disorder or imperfected nature of things. All this reflects a life based on the establishment of some form of being rooted in the attaching or clinging phenomenon. This form of being is best illustrated by Buddhism as maintaining or perpetuating what is known in Sanskrit as *ātman*, a self-oriented view or perception. It is a self-serving view, for it channels all elements of perception for its own benefit.

It can be seen that the states or natures of ignorance, desire, rebirth, and sorrow must be destroyed or extinguished in order for one to discharge one's proper functions among other persons with tolerance, forbearance, and brotherly and sisterly love "without distinction," including kindness to members of the animal kingdom. The former set of states and the latter set of traits are really two aspects of the same reality. They are aspects of human existence in that, where the former educes the worst in a person, the latter educes the best or finest. A new perspective of being is advanced, one which the historical Buddha discovered in his enlightenment. It can be attained by anyone, of course, but the regimen is so strict and taxing that only a gifted few are able to go all the way and realize this novel perspective. The "content" of this perspective, or the nature of enlightenment, is the key to understanding the virtuous traits which we associate with or relate to fellow creatures, including animals. Thus tolerance, forbearance, brotherly and sisterly love, and kindness are actually expressions which relate to the enlightened realm of existence.

The question that immediately arises is what all this has to do with human rights. Human rights is indeed an important issue, but the Buddhist position is that it is ancillary to the larger or more basic issue of human nature.

It can be asserted that the Buddhist sees the concept of human rights as a legal extension of human nature. It is a crystallization, indeed a formalization, of the mutual respect and concern of all persons, stemming from human nature. Thus, human nature is the ultimate source, the basis from which all other attributes or characteristics are to be delineated. They all have their respective *raison d'etre* in it. They are reflections and even by-products of it. The reason for assigning human nature the basic position is very simple. It is to give human relations a firm grounding in the truly existential nature of things: that is, the concrete and dynamic relational nature of persons in contact with each other, that which avoids being caught up in rhetorical or legalistic tangles.

For example, Article 3 of the Universal Declaration of Human Rights states: "Everyone has the right to life, liberty and the security of person." This is a noble statement and a well-thought-out declaration. Yet, from the Buddhist standpoint, the concepts of "right" to life, liberty, and the security of person address the individual in an unclear way. It is unclear because it speaks first of life and the person, but then it speaks of liberty and security and attempts to relate the latter to the former in rather abstract terms. It does not speak of the ambience in which the concepts or conditions are to exist and take effect. So, while the Article itself is an excellent statement of the sanctity of the individual person, its effectiveness and persuasiveness are wanting. It lacks the sustaining power and the cogency which apply to all situations or circumstances—large or small, significant or insignificant, domestic or foreign.

It should be pointed out that the Buddhist does not want to be caught up in peripheral accounting in dealing with or defining the intrinsic nature of life and the individual. There must be direct and more intimate bonds that bind life-process itself in terms of other lives in the specific and general relationships. Consequently, the Buddhist concern is focused on the experiential process of each individual, a process technically known as relational origination (*paticca-samuppāda*). It is the great doctrine of Buddhism, perhaps the greatest doctrine expounded by the historical Buddha. It means that, in any life-process, the arising of an experiential event is a total, relational affair. A particular event does not arise in a vacuum, nor does it result by the imposition of external forces or elements. It is a unique arisal which is vitally dependent on or related to all the elements present within the surroundings. Thus, in the process there is nothing which is fragmentary or has any gaps, since it relates with the complete fullness of all the elements present. Each relationship is full insofar as the process is concerned. This means that relational origination is a most concrete way in which life-process goes on.

Like a storm which consumes everything in its wake, an experience in terms of relational origination involves everything within its purview. Hence, the involvement of elements and, in our case, human beings as entities should be not in terms of mere relationship but rather a creative relationship which originates from the individual locus of existence. In other words, each individual is responsible for the actualization of an "extensive concern" for everything that lies in his or her path of experience. So, we may say that the sum total of the "extensive concerns" can be referred to as a mutually constituted existential realm, and it thereby becomes a fact that there will be mutual respect of fellow beings. It is on this basis that we can speak of the rights of individuals. These rights are actually extensions of human qualities such as security, liberty, and life.

The onus of the extensive concern is on the individual, because he or she is the very dynamic, creative locus of existence. And that locus of existence is not a permanent entity but a constant co-extensive and co-originating phenomenon. In any given situation or ambience, the loci must meet harmoniously; otherwise, there will be mere physical contact which does not elevate the relationship to the nonphysical, exalted feeling which stems principally from the respective loci. In a figurative sense, then, one can picture a whole field of loci touching each other and relating to each other in such a way that each essence of being is permitted to sustain itself. The sustenance is perpetuated in virtue of the fact that each being, in and of itself, is an instance of the dynamic relational origination.

What has just been described is difficult to discern, but it is not beyond our understanding. After all, it was the genius of the Buddha to perceive the profound way in which the experiential process goes on and in which the whole field of experiences comes into play. The Buddha saw that the norm of existence belongs to the norm of experiential process or relational origination. This norm in its deepest sense is what the Buddha referred to as the "Dhamma" (Sanskrit: *Dharma*). It is the vision of truth. Indeed, "Dhamma" is another name for the truth of existence, the real nature in which experiences go on. It is, of course, the enlightened way of life. Thus, the Buddha asserted: "He who sees relational origination sees the *Dhamma* and he who sees the *Dhamma* sees relational origination."[6]

Here the enlightened nature (Buddha) and the experiential process (relational origination) collapse. Indeed, these two realms can also be identified with the Dhamma, the true norm of existence. The capture or vision of this norm of existence naturally entails a rigorous meditative discipline. We cannot expect this discipline to go its route for everyone; however, we can aspire for that ideal existence by seeking and actualizing the proper relationship among human beings and beyond—that is, inclusive of the elements of the rest of the surrounding world. In the case under review, it is the study of human nature and its extension to the realm of human rights. In consequence, there is an intimate and vital relationship of the Buddhist norm or Dhamma with that of human rights.

---

[6]*Majjhima-nikāya*, I, 190-191. *The Collection of the Middle Length Sayings*, trans. I. B. Horner (London: Luzac & Co., 1954), vol. 1, pp. 236-237.

Let me pursue the Buddhist approach further. I wrote above of the "extensive concern." This is the locus of individual existence which extends over to and harmonizes with other loci of existence. This extensive nature, which takes into consideration or involves the total loci of existence, is thoroughly holistic; yet, it is holistic in the sense that it neither asserts nor denies the nature of the individual. This is a subtle point which needs elaboration.

For example, we have used the concept of the individual to refer to an independently existing entity in and from which everything occurs. That is, it has been used to depict the subject or the self which engages in all forms of activity, and thus it becomes the focal point, the originator, and the final fruit of all experiences. All that seems simple enough, yet in Buddhism all references to the subject, self, or individuality are categorically denied. The denial usually comes as a shock for early initiates to Buddhism. Why is this so? Because the denial will mean the end of individuality and individual existence? A good reply, perhaps, but profoundly incorrect. The Buddhist position is that, contrary to the accepted interpretation of the individual or self, these concepts will take on deeper meaning and nature by focusing on the holistic nature of things.

To be a self, in short, means to extend beyond itself. This is paradoxical, but on closer examination it will be acknowledged that the life-process is not merely a steady, locus-limited function. A self which asserts itself—for example, in mere discrimination, selection, acceptance, rejection, forestalling, anticipation, controlling, commanding, etc.—does not know that it is, by so functioning, basically fragmenting or truncating itself. All this is common practice and knowledge, but the "common" nature is subject to review here. In fact, the Buddha, prior to his enlightenment, experienced the same phenomenon of fragmentation of the self, that is, he realized the dichotomous nature. After his enlightenment, he enunciated his famous doctrine of anatman (Pali: *anattā*) or "non-self," turning the whole posture of existence upside down or inside out, and heralding the new Buddhist era. This doctrine of anatman is, of course, in contrast to the prevailing doctrine of atman (Pali: *attā*) or "self" promulgated by the orthodox Hindus.

Much debate has been generated in pitting the atman against anatman. In all fairness to both Buddhists and Hindus, it must be cautioned that neither doctrine is grist for the conceptual mill. These are not logical entities or objects, nor are they logical opposites. Each depicts a unique existential phenomenon which must be understood within its own perspectival framework: the atman within the Brahmanic context, and the anatman within the Dharma or Dhammic context.

What the Buddha has done is to point out that the ordinary self which we accept is really a limiting concept which closes the doors for the realization of an open existential nature. In contrast, the non-self is without limits and, therefore, by its very nature, reveals an open existential nature. Though all this seems vague, or perhaps even strange and bizarre, the reality of our experiential process is potentially of this character. Without the openness, the experiential process would be limited in scope and, worst of all, it would be largely deterministic. The limitedness or narrowness of the process would mean less free play of entities and would result in much of repetitive or habitual functions. But is not this what much of our ordinary experience has fallen into? Is not this one of the bases for noncreative activities?

In sum, the anatman doctrine is a challenge to break out of the shell of individual ontology. This does not mean to destroy the ordinary concept of the self but rather to assert its true nature by ridding it of its individuating characteristics. It is to open up the individual locus of existence so as to involve other loci of existence. In this way, there is an ambience of open ontology which fosters the actualization of a truly holistic nature of existence. The support of the ambience of an open ontology must naturally be a mutually cooperative affair. In this way we are able to appreciate the greater extensive realm of existence in which we basically live and thrive. The thrust into the greater realm can only come from individuals who sense the limitations of ordinary selfhood and are thus willing to open up and engage other selves and their existential natures. When a sufficient number of individuals are engaged in this fashion, there will exist the mutuality of concern and respect which are the hallmarks of the preservation and continuity of human existence. Otherwise, the struggle for existence based on the self or ego can and will go unchecked and will ultimately end in disorder, usurpation, and the total destruction of humankind.

Buddhist teachings always center on the imperfect nature of the self and aim at its alleviation by showing the delimiting factors. Seen in this light, the teachings take on deeper meaning and significance. They aim at universal application and cogency. For example, look at the five standard Buddhist moral precepts (pañcaśīla): (1) abstain from killing any living being; (2) abstain from stealing; (3) abstain from unlawful sexual intercourse; (4) abstain from lying; and (5) abstain from the use of intoxicants.[7] In any language, the precepts are simple enough to understand. In fact, other traditions have similar or identical proscriptions on misconduct.

However, when these precepts are examined in the context of the individual in relationship to other ontologies, they take on new insights. That is to say, they force the individual and his or her ontology to open up or extend to other ontologies. For example, stealing or lying immediately brings forth to the individual concerned the possessive individuating characteristics which deny the ontologies of others, the result being that the prevailing harmony or harmonious relationship is sundered. However, when stealing or lying is nonexistent, the ontological harmony is sustained through mutual extensive concern. Thus, in the *Sigālovāda-sutta* the Buddha exhorts:

---

[7]*Sāmañña-phala Sutta*, 17. "The Fruits of the Life of a Recluse," in *Dialogues of the Buddha*, Part I, *Sāmañña-phala Suttanta*, trans. T. W. Rhys Davids (London: Luzac & Co., 1956), p. 69.

Who transgresses the Doctrine [i.e., Dhamma] through passion, hatred, fear or delusion, his fame [i.e., reputation] wanes like the moon in the dark half of the month.

Who transgresses not the Doctrine through passion, hatred, fear or delusion, his fame waxes full like the moon in the light half of the month.[8]

The passage clearly indicates that the Doctrine or Dhamma is the focus and that any deviation from it would result in disgrace or blemish of one's nature. But, if the Dhamma is followed closely and if one's experiential process is in tune with the Dhamma, then one's nature will grow or nourish fully. In short, the exhortation clearly places the responsibility for the nourishment of one's inner nature on the individual and treats the relationship of the inner nature and the concern of others as continuous. The Dhamma is the key; it is that which gathers all or that which brings all ontologies into a coherent whole.

The holistic nature is one which we have potentially. It requires a mutuality of ontologies in the form of good friends. Thus, the same sutra goes on to promote friendship on the most intimate and lasting basis. It speaks of four types of good-at-heart friends: "The friend who is a help, the friend who is the same in happiness and pain, the friend who shows what is profitable and the friend who has compassion."[9] Again, looked upon from the standpoint of self and other ontologies, we can appreciate the openness with which the ontologies intersect. A good, trusted friend epitomizes the supremacy of ontological extensive nature under which one is the beneficiary. It firms up the relationship "internally," within the context of the total relational field.

The above discussion on sound friendship and the reality of the extensive nature brings us finally to the great contribution of Buddhism—the doctrine of Bodhisattva. Literally, "Bodhisattva" means the enlightened being or the nature of a perfected being. But the Bodhisattva is also referred to as the "would-be Buddha," which in turn can be interpreted as signifying the fact that everyone can aspire to tread the enlightened path and, indeed, could even become a Buddha. This is not to denigrate Buddhahood or even Bodhisattvahood but in truth to exhibit the potentiality and access to taking up the faith and disciplinary practice.

Perhaps the most basic nature is that Bodhisattvas seek enlightenment not only for themselves but for others.[10] They constantly think of the welfare or well-being of others. They even postpone their own nirvana, because they vow not to enter it until or unless all sentient creatures have been brought before it. Here we see the capping of the nature of universal concern, that is, the extensive

---

[8]Translation from Edward J. Thomas, *Early Buddhist Scriptures* (London: Kegan Paul, Trench, Trubner & Co., 1935), p. 144.

[9]Ibid., p. 147.

[10]See, e.g., Har Dayal's meticulous study, *The Bodhisattva Doctrine in Buddhist Sanskrit Literature* (London: Kegan Paul, Trench, Trubner & Co., 1932), pp. 1-29.

nature of a supreme being whose very nature is to bring warmth, security, regard, and salvation to all. In a sweeping way the Bodhisattva way has brought all ontologies together, because each and every creature in the world, including nonhumans, is involved in its very constitution. It is an all-or-nothing affair, undergirded by infinite patience and compassion. As a matter of fact, the Bodhisattva is one who possesses the dual nature of wisdom (*prajñā*) and compassion (*karuṇā*), which are, in many respects, two aspects of the same reality of a perfected being. That is, an all-knowing person must necessarily be an all-loving person, and an all-loving person must necessarily be an all-knowing person. This fact shows that intelligence and practice ideally must coincide at all times. It also shows that an intelligent act is not only intensive but also extensive, that is, the penetrative knowledge is clear, but simultaneously it goes beyond individualistic (limited) designs. In fact, the act at the same time must always be open for the involvement of others. Consequently, the act becomes a great act of tremendous proportions.

Concluding Remarks

I began with the statement that the world is becoming either smaller or larger, depending on one's interpretation of the shifts and changes which are occurring in the world. While the shifts and changes are real factors which come into play as the years go by, it is still important to be able to perceive certain lasting aspects of humankind which would at least give us a reliable focus and a means by which to secure an understanding of human relations. From the obvious reality of individual existence we must move on to greater spheres of social existence and to the idealized pluralistic ontological realm. It is here that the Bodhisattva concept offers a challenge.

The Bodhisattva personifies the ideality of existence, not only on a personal basis but also in the larger social or world context. It exhibits the highest level human beings can achieve, singly as well as collectively. In its concern for fellow beings, it demonstrates the best concrete illustration of the doctrine of relational origination—in which every being is involved in every other being in the dynamic, experiential process. The process is necessarily an enlightening one because of the basic extensive concern which reaches out into the surrounding world. It is not only the beginnings of harmony with other beings but, more important, the sustenance of harmony within the changing ambient world.

The Bodhisattva ideal speaks to us of equality, liberty, and security from the total perspective. Therefore, its reference to human nature is at once on the greater social level, for social nature can be interpreted as an agglomeration of individual human nature. In this way, equality, liberty, and security are enhanced from the holistic nature of things. Indeed, these qualities are meaningful and persuasive only to the extent that they belong to the greater realm of existence. Put another way, these qualities are meaningless and impotent when applied to a single individual, for an individual without the social bindings is simply incomprehensible, or at least is in such a singular state of existence that those qualities do not apply. The extensive, social, and pluralistic characteristics are inherent in those qualities; they are the marks of universality.

Finally, to return to the central question of human rights: the Buddhist perspective has shown that it goes directly to the heart of human nature. Indeed, the former is only an extension of the latter. In other words, it cannot go the other way around; the status of human nature cannot be sought in human rights. Human rights are legal matters which can be legislated, but only to a certain extent, especially so in a divided world. Human nature, however, is an existential matter which can neither be legislated nor measured; therefore, one must resort to persuasion and self-realization in order to seek one's unique existence. Although human nature crosses national boundaries in terms of human-to-human contacts, much of this is mired in governmental intervention or interference. But when governments, singly or in consortium, are able to provide an ambience conducive to individual life-fulfillment by way of an open and free contact to all, the question of human rights based on human nature should be eased considerably, if not solved. That would be the Buddhist option.

7.

HUMAN RIGHTS IN HINDUISM

Kana Mitra

A discussion on human rights in Hinduism, like a discussion on almost any religious issue, needs some preliminary statements to clarify its scope and method, since religion, like sex, is a subject that easily generates misunderstanding and controversy. Any discussion of Hinduism in general terms is difficult because of the enormous variety and plurality within this tradition. Hinduism has no single text which is of ultimate authority, no institutional hierarchy like that of the Roman Catholic Church which can be referred to as a source of authority, and no common form of behavior among all Hindus which represents a common consensus. Both critics of and apologists for Hinduism can use various sources selectively to justify their views. For a scholarly discussion of Hinduism, then, each author needs to indicate clearly the sources which form the basis of the discussion and also the rationale for selecting some sources rather than others.

In this essay the discussion on human rights is based primarily on Manu's *Dharma Sūtra*. The rationale for this selection is threefold. First, in Hinduism the correct form of practice is more important than correct formulation of beliefs. The codes of praxis are found in the *Dharma Sāstras*.[1] Manu's *Dharma Sūtra* is considered authoritative by tradition-oriented Hindus. Manu's code upholds the hierarchical social order of Hinduism, which seems to be incompatible with the idea of human rights. This allows us to focus on the negative aspect of Hinduism regarding human rights. Second, from as early as the fifth century B.C. down to the present, there have been frequent rebellions against the hierarchical social order of Hinduism. Many reformers have rejected Manu's *Dharma Sūtra*. However, most tradition-oriented Hindus, including Mahatma Gandhi, are of the opinion that, although Manu's code is not acceptable in its entirety to contemporary Hindu society, it can yet contribute to the establishing of a just society. Thus, discussion on the basis of Manu will enable a focus on the positive aspect of Hinduism regarding human rights. Third, present-day Hindu society, despite its many changes and transformations, still shows Manu's influence. The

---

[1]There are various *Dharma Sutras* associated with various authors: *Gautama Dharma Sutra*, *Baudhyana Dharma Sutra*, *Apasthambha Dharma Sutra*, etc.

Kana Mitra (Hindu) is an Adjunct Professor of Religion at LaSalle College and Villanova University. A native of India, she earned an M.A. in philosophy at the University of Calcutta and a Ph.D. in Religion at Temple University. She has written for the *Journal of Ecumenical Studies* and the forthcoming *Offenbarung als Heilserfahrung in Christentum, Hinduismus und Buddhismus*.

Hindu Code Bill adopted by the Indian Parliament in the middle of this century was influenced by Manu.[2]

If we look in the dictionary for a Sanskrit equivalent for the word "right," we notice that the suggested Sanskrit words do not have the precise connotation of "right" as it is used in the Universal Declaration of Human Rights.[3] Of course, the Declaration was not adopted from a religious perspective. Developed in a context of secular, individualistic, and democratic values, it may not be meaningful in the context of a socio-political order which has traditionally been hierarchical. Many scholars, therefore, are reluctant to discuss the issue of human rights from the perspective of Hinduism.

This view has its justification, which is no doubt evident in various interreligious dialogues which end up in either monologues or debate because the same term has different meanings in different contexts. A familiar example is the word "Messiah" in the Jewish-Christian dialogue. Another is the condemnation of Hinduism as idolatrous, pantheistic, or nonmoral by some Christian scholars who misunderstand the context of image worship or the idea of *Brahman* or *Mokṣa* from a Western, Christian perspective. However, just as many people today feel the urgent need for dialogue between different religions, many people also feel the pressing need for dialogue between religious and nonreligious ideas, between religious and secular concerns. Many modern Hindus value democracy and individualism. They need to discover whether these values are incompatible with Hinduism.

Some serious scholars suggest that in order to obviate these difficulties of terms and contexts it is useful to define words in terms of their intentionality and not simply literally and philologically.[4] It can then be seen whether the same intentionality is present in other traditions, even if the same literal word is not used.[5] Following this suggestion will reveal that "right" as it is used in the Declaration means a claim which is in accord with justice and propriety. Of course, the words "justice" and "propriety" are themselves not univocal, as is evident in Plato's *Republic* or Confucius' *Li Chi*. Yet, justice and propriety in the context of secular, individualistic, and democratic values imply egalitarianism, equal concern for all humans.

The Sanskrit word "*adhikāra*" also has the meaning of a just claim. However, discussion of the idea of human rights in terms of *adhikāra* cannot go very

---

[2]J. Duncan M. Derrett, *Introduction to Modern Hindu Law* (Bombay: Oxford University Press, 1963).

[3]See pp. 105-109, below.

[4]Many Catholic thinkers in dialogue with Hinduism suggest "dialogue of intentionality." E.g., Henri Le Saux (Abhisiktananda) suggested that the dialogue takes place in "the cave of heart" (*Hindu-Christian Meeting Point* [Delhi: Indian Society for the Promotion of Christhan Knowledge, 1976]); also see K. Klostermaier, "Hindu-Christian Dialogue," *Journal of Ecumenical Studies* 5 (1968): 21-44.

[5]Raimundo Panikkar indicated the similarity of intention between Christ of Christianity and *Īśvara* of Hinduism, although their philological meanings are not alike, in *The Unknown Christ of Hinduism* (London: Darton, Longman and Todd, 1964), especially the last chapter.

far. Manu uses the term *adhikāra* in a positive way mostly in reference to the Brahmans, and not regarding others.[6] Manu's code would thus suggest that Hinduism advocates only the rights of the Brahmans, not the rights of all humans. The history of Hinduism to a certain extent would also justify this view.

One must beware, however, of making hasty conclusions. As codes of conduct, *Dharma Sūtras* emphasize more the duties of humans than their rights; the word *"adhikāra"* thus does not occur frequently. Like most other religions of the world, Hinduism emphasizes the duties of humans rather than their rights. Duties and rights being interrelated, it is possible to formulate ideas about rights from ideas about duties. *Dharma Sūtras* use the term *"dharma"* more frequently than *adhikāra*. *Dharma* implies justice and propriety as does the word "right" of the U.N. declaration, although the connotation of a "just claim" is not explicitly present. Yet, since *dharma* is the closest equivalent to "right," I shall attempt to explore human rights in Hinduism in terms of *dharma*.

Manu's code is called *Manava Dharma Sūtra* (The Treatise on Human Duties).[7] Although the name refers to humans, people's duties and rights are specified not in terms of their humanity but in terms of specific caste, age, and sex.[8]

The Hindu caste system is the hierarchical social structure in which people belonging to different castes have neither the same duties nor the same privileges.[9] Although in reality there are almost innumerable castes, ideally, and as presented in the codes, there are four castes. The Brahman or priestly and teaching caste has the duty of acquiring and spreading knowledge. Brahmans are the keepers of the Vedas; they are exempt from working for their sustenance. The Kshatriya or kingly and warrior caste has the duty of protecting people from criminal and political dangers. Members have the privilege of sharing the Brahmans' knowledge and Vaisyas' wealth, as well as the service of the Sudras. The Vaisya or producing and cultivating caste has the duty of generating and distributing wealth. Members have the privilege of sharing the Brahmans' knowledge, the Kshatriyas' protection, and the Sudras' service. The Sudras have the duty of serving all. They are entitled to the Kshatriyas' protection and Vaisyas' wealth, but they are denied the right to share the Brahmans' wisdom. Besides

---

[6]Manu uses the word *"Adhikāra"* in the context of Brahmanas—e.g., 1:100—in a positive sense, but in the context of women—e.g., 9:3—in a negative way.

[7]For the history of Manu's *Dharma Sutra*, see Georg Bühler, *The Laws of Manu* (New York: Dover, 1969), pp. xi-cvi.

[8]In Manu there are some general rules of conduct for all humans; e.g., 8:350 suggests that any human can slay an assassin, yet punishment against adultery is different for different castes; e.g., 8:359 indicates that anyone except a Brahmana should suffer death for such an offense.

[9]For the caste system, see Kana Mitra, "Caste in India," in P. K. Meagher, ed., *Encyclopedic Dictionary of Religion* (Washington, DC: Corpus Publications, 1979); and V. P. Varma, "Studies in Hindu Political Thought and Its Metaphysical Foundation," *The Journal of Bihar Research Society* 38 (March, 1952): 69-78.

these four castes there developed the category of outcastes, or untouchables, who had none of the above caste privileges. The caste system seems to be wholly incompatible with the idea of human rights.

In Manu, rights and duties are related not only to caste but also to age. The usual span of human life in the ancient Hindu texts is 100 years. Life is seen as divided into four equal divisions or stages of twenty-five years each. First is the period of studentship (*Brahmacarya*) when the duty is to cultivate discipline and learning. Then comes the period of householdership (*Gārhasthya*) in which the duty is creation of wealth, success, and family. The next is the stage of withdrawal (*Vānaprastha*), when the duty is to detach oneself from worldly pursuits for the sake of the spiritual. The final stage is renunciation (*Sanyāsa*), in which all duties are finally transcended, and there is total equanimity. In this final stage the Hindu has no caste and is not bound by the duties of caste.

Like caste and age, sex plays an important part in determining one's rights and duties. The roles of male and female in Manu's code are considered as interdependent, yet they are not equal. Manu IX, 3, is often quoted to indicate the perpetual dependence of women on men.[10] Manu IX, 76, contrasted with IX, 77, seems no less discriminatory.[11]

The code of Manu appears to be propagating and upholding the inequality of humans and, hence, injustice. It is contrary to human rights. That people revolted against this hierarchical order is not surprising. Several tendencies can be noticed in these rebellions. First, there is a tendency to separate from Hinduism and offer an alternative religion. Buddhism and Jainism in the fifth century B.C. and Sikhism in the fifteenth century A.D. are examples. Second, it is possible to separate from Hinduism but offer nonreligious alternatives. The *Lokayatas*, or popularists, for example, do not believe in any ultimate meaning for human existence. They denounce all religious codes of conduct and, like the *Cārvāskas*, live a life in pursuit of pleasure or, like the *Ājivakas*, live a life of asceticism to minimize the pains of life. Third, some groups remain within Hinduism but enact reforms. Some *bhakti* groups denied Manu's hierarchical social order,[12] but most of them do not denounce the caste system totally. All humans are equal as God's creation but are not the same; therefore, all should

---

[10]Manu 9:3: "Her father protects [her] in childhood, her husband protects [her] in youth, and her sons protect [her] in old age: a woman is never fit for independence" (Bühler, *Laws of Manu*, p. 328).

[11]Manu 9:76: "If a husband went abroad for some sacred duty, [she] must wait for him eight years, if [he went] to [acquire] learning or fame six [years], if [he went] for pleasure three years." Manu 9:77: "For one year let a husband bear the wife who hates him; but after [the lapse of] a year let him deprive her of her property and cease to cohabit with her" (ibid., p. 341).

[12]Chaitanya (fifteenth century), the vaishnava saint, was against the caste system in any form. Alvars (eighth century), also a vaishnava, did not recognize any caste distinctions. Among ten recognized saints of the alvars, some were sudras, some outcastes, and one was a woman. The virashivas (twelfth century), belonging to the shiva group in its early period, accepted caste distinctions but later discarded them.

give and receive according to their own nature. These groups uphold the idea of following one's own nature (*svadharma*) as advocated in the *Bhagavad-Gītā*. Although some contemporary scholars of Hinduism[13] find some incompatibility between the idea of following one's own nature and the idea of perennial and eternal truth (*sanātana dharma*), as advocated in different forms of Hinduism in general and the *Bhagavad-Gītā* in particular, most of the Hindu devotional schools think that the first is a means to the second.

The various vedanta groups[14] are within the limits of Hindu orthodoxy. They uphold human rights on the basis of all human beings' having the same essence. *Advaita Vedānta* advocates the nonduality of the essence of humans and the divine. Like other classical vedanta schools, it still believes in Manu's hierarchy. Humans may be potentially divine, yet in actual life they do not actualize this potentiality in the same degree. One should, therefore, follow one's own nature or *svadharma* to realize the perennial, eternal truth.

In the nineteenth and twentieth centuries, the encounter with Western individualistic and democratic values evoked various reform movements in Hinduism. These movements for human rights are in line with the U.N. declaration. Some of these reformers, such as Gandhi, have influenced all subsequent thinkers. Rammohan Roy, the founder of the Brahma Samaj movement, advocates equality of all humans irrespective of caste or sex. He wants a total elimination of Hinduism's hierarchical social system. He rejects Manu on the ground that his text belongs to the category of tradition and not of revelation. The revealed texts of Hinduism, the Vedas and Upanishads, advocate the equality of all humans. Rammohan Roy, as a monotheist, bases his idea of equality on the fact that all humans are God's creatures.

Vivekananda, the founder of the Ramakrishna Movement, advocates equality on the basis of Vedanta. The essence of all humans is divine; hence, all are children of divinity. He does not, however, denounce Manu. His argument is the usual vedantic argument: humans are equal in essence, but in actual life situations they are different and distinct. Hierarchy, according to him, can be a source of protection rather than discrimination. The right to the free movement of a person in a wheelchair can be protected only if his or her difference from the person able to walk is recognized.

Rabindranath Tagore is another influential name in the human-rights movement. His father belonged to Rammohan's Brahma Samaj; however, Rabindranath's contribution was more as a poet with a universal vision than as a member of Brahma Samaj. Although he is a monotheist, his primary concern is human-

---

[13]See R. C. Zaehner, *Hinduism* (London: Oxford University Press, 1962), especially chaps. 5, 7, and 8; and Norbert Klaes, *Conscience and Consciousness*, No. 15 (Bangalore: Dharmaram Publications, 1975).

[14]Among the ten schools of vedanta, the advaita vedanta of Shamkara and the vishistadvaita of Ramanuja are better known. Advaita vedanta is usually considered to be nontheistic because of its nonpersonalistic understanding of the divine. All the other schools are theistic, insofar as they recognize a personal God.

ism. His *Religion of Man* gives a theoretical understanding of his view, and the university which he established at Shantiniketana in the early part of this century, which is still flourishing, exemplifies his ideal.

These are but a few of the leaders and thinkers who advocate human rights in Hinduism. Mahatma Gandhi is the epitome of the human-rights movement from within traditional Hinduism. His continuous struggle against untouchability and for the improvement of the conditions of the outcastes was the most important motivation of his life. This fight for the rights of the untouchables was based on his idea of human rights. Gandhi wrote:

> Men are equal. For, though they are not of the same age, same height, the same skin and the same intellect, these inequalities are temporary and superficial, the soul that is hidden beneath this earthly crust is one and the same for all men and women belonging to all climes. . . . The word "inequality" has a bad odour to it, and it has led to arrogance and inhumanities, both in East and West.[15]

Gandhi indicated here that the idea of superiority and inferiority is contrary to Hindu theology. Gandhi considered himself an orthodox Hindu. He had the vision of a personal as well as a supra-personal divinity. As a devotee of Rama, Gandhi used to sing that he who is Rama is also Rahima; *Allah* and *Iśvara* are not two. But, although we envision God as a person, too much emphasis on person can become restrictive. So Gandhi often stated that God is Truth. He believed that, whether theistic or nontheistic, no form of Hindu theology justified an inequality of humans. Theistic Hinduism upholds human equality on the basis that all are God's creatures. Nontheistic Hinduism emphasizes the identity of the essence of all humans.

However, Gandhi did accept Manu's idea of differing rights and duties. He said that what a Brahman can do an outcaste cannot do, and vice versa. He was even willing to accept the superiority of a Brahman insofar as it implied some qualities of the individual and not a status by birth. A Brahman is a lover of truth, friend of all, unselfish, nonviolent, humble. Thus, Manu justifies Gandhi.[16] But for a Brahman to claim superiority is to forfeit the claim. Gandhi indicated that today among the Hindus there are no Brahmans. All are Sudras. We Hindus forfeited our claim to study the Vedas, as Vedas cannot be understood by intellect alone. Gandhi was a true vedantin in this respect. The primary text of Vedānta, the *Brahma Sūtra*, indicates that some prerequisites need to be fulfilled before the inquiry about *Brahman*.[17] In the various yogic practices, too, the elimination of immoral qualities (*Yama*) and the cultivation of moral virtues (*Niyama*) are considered to be prerequisites for the pursuit of truth.

---

[15]Mohandas K. Gandhi, *None High, None Low*, ed. and pub., Anand T. Hingorani (Bombay: Bharatiya Vidya Bhavan, 1975), p. 2.

[16]Manu 2:87, 155-168, etc.

[17]*Brahma Sutra* 1.1.1.

This review of the history of human rights according to traditional Hinduism indicates one important characteristic: a recognition of plurality and distinctiveness, together with the equality of all human beings. The idea of rights and duties according to one's station in life (*Varnāśrama dharma*), which is advocated in the Hindu tradition as presented by Manu, has many discriminatory attitudes, and in the history of Hinduism it led to injustice and inhumanity. That is why the view of Western critics such as Hegel and Burckhardt that the caste system of Hinduism is the strongest negation of individuality is justified.[18] But the views of such apologists as Radhakrishnan and R. P. Masani that caste is an attempt at balance between extreme individualism and extreme collectivism is also justified.[19]

According to Manu, one's *dharma* or duties and rights need to be understood in terms of *svadharma*, or according to one's natural aptitude and situation in life. One's capacity in a certain stage of life or in a certain situation is of a certain specific type. Again, an individual's rights and duties cannot be determined from the perspective of the individual alone; one's relationship with others also needs to be considered. In the name of human rights, sometimes individualism is let loose, and the consequence is unbridled "me-ism." The restraints of the Hindu caste system may be considered as an antidote. The idea of *svadharma*, if not understood as a rigid code or law, can be a contribution in the field of human rights in its suggestion that differences be taken seriously. Manu offers suggestions in taking it in a nonrigid way. *Dharma*, he says, is what "is followed by those learned of the Vedas and what is approved by the conscience of the virtuous who are exempt from hatred and inordinate affection."[20] Tradition, conscience, and reason must all be consulted to determine the rights and duties of humans. Rights and duties of different people in different situations are different, but each human being deserves and should have equal consideration and equal concern.

But understanding aptitude and potential in terms of birth is bound to produce injustice. It is true that each individual's aptitude and inclination are of a specific nature at a particular time, but what guarantee is there that they are necessarily reflected in one's caste by birth? There are obvious biological differences between male and female, but what guarantee is there that they necessarily determine the potential for actual activities of life? Elders are obviously more mature in age, but what guarantee is there that they are necessarily more mature in wisdom?

---

[18]Georg Wilhelm Friedrich Hegel, *Philosophy of Right*, trans. with notes by T. M. Knox (Chicago: Encyclopaedia Britannica, 1955); and Jakob Christoph Burckhardt, *Force and Freedom: Reflections on History*, ed. James Hastings Nichols (New York: Pantheon Books, 1943).

[19]Radhakrishnan, *The Hindu View of Life* (London: George Allen and Unwin, 1961); R. P. Masani, "Caste and the Structure of Society," in G. T. Garratt, ed., *The Legacy of India* (Oxford: Clarendon Press, 1937).

[20]Manu 2:1.

The hierarchical social order of Hinduism has the merit of acknowledging human differences seriously; thus, it can act as a protection of each individual's rights by eliminating what is often unhealthy and unjust competition. In traditional Hinduism these human differences are considered to be hereditary, because birth, according to Hinduism, is not an accident but is the result of actions in one's past life. Thus, birth in a particular caste or as a particular sex is dependent on one's previous life. This idea of reincarnation is intimately related to the law of *karma*, or the law of action and reaction.

Hindu reformers have not as yet critically discussed these theoretical bases for social hierarchy. Some would like to reject social hierarchy because it is a source of injustice, but they remain unsuccessful. Some tradition-oriented Hindus, such as Gandhi, believe such a rejection would disintegrate Hinduism. Gandhi did not want to accept superiority or inferiority dependent on birth—yet he did not suggest any alternative for determination of caste. It seems that he, too, accepted uncritically the nonaccidental determination of birth by reincarnation and the law of karma.

It is evident that the establishment of human rights among Hindus demands not only social reform movements, but also exploration, investigation, and reinterpretation of the theoretical foundations underlying the social hierarchy of Hinduism.

8.

A SOCIAL HISTORIAN RESPONDS

Dennis J. Clark

It is refreshing to read these engagements of questing minds with the fundamental problems of human-rights definition and explication derived from theological traditions. The task of seeking unity of commitment to human rights—
a unity of commitment which transcends all the political, legal, and controversial
obstacles—is of paramount importance when destruction of lives and the ravag-
ing of human values rage through various societies across the globe.

From the viewpoint of the sociologist and the social historian, the essays
reveal notable problems of religious and theological discontinuity which profoundly compromise the relation of theology to the manifold needs to develop
coherence and intellectual influence in order to strengthen human-rights safeguards. Both as an abstract discipline and as a summons to holiness and to
brotherhood and sisterhood, theology has a pivotal role to play in elevating
human consciousness and behavior. For the leadership of societies influenced by
formal religion it has a crucial formative and activating role as a discipline and as
a basis for social ideals. The contributions of the various religious traditions set
forth in these essays are an encouraging testimony to the fruits of scholarship
and religious awareness. The discontinuity even within single traditions and the
shortcomings of the traditions in vindicating their historic missions, however,
deeply undercut their proclamations of universal validity and pertinence to
human suffering and the need for a humane order in the world.

Each of the great religious traditions arises out of some cultural current,
each with varying cycles of eminence and creativity. Some of these cultural
currents are epochal in scope and extend into various ranges of antiquity. It is
this antiquity, this historical evolution through different social contexts, that has
produced negations and defaults in the witness of these traditions to human
rights. The different scriptural traditions are compromised by the cultural
adumbrations, ambiguities, and linguistic limitations that surround their expression of divine wisdom and instruction. The classification of human persons
according to historically and culturally conditioned views of status, inclusion
and exclusion, sexual taboos, and doctrinal prescriptions occludes the obligation
to embrace all humanity in an age of global communication and exchange. The
disparity among the religious traditions poses complex problems for the deriva-
tion of a supra-national ethic which will set standards for the protection of
human rights across diverse legal and cultural barriers.

Dennis J. Clark (Roman Catholic) is the Executive Director of the Samuel S. Fels Fund,
a charitable foundation in Philadelphia. He received both his M.A. and Ph.D. in history
from Temple University. Among his books are *The Getto Game* and *The Irish Relations:
Trials of an Immigrant Tradition*.

The problems of the scriptural traditions, the gaps in protections of rights because of inequities, the preoccupations of various religious codes with ritual and ephemeral and culturally dispensible and changeable factors: all these things divert the traditions from the central consideration of assuring humans of the dignity they require as creatures of God. Stanley Harakas asserts clearly the problems of scripture. Daniel Polish boldly confirms the difficulty of traditional denial of full religious and social status to women. The Roman Catholic and Protestant traditions both bear severe handicaps in their historical records of religious absolutism in different times and places, yet, as John Langan notes, there is an obligation to strive for the implementation of human rights. Such inherited anachronisms as those related to slavery noted by Riffat Hassan and the problems of caste interpretation alluded to by Kana Mitra do not diminish this obligation. In the modern period with its impulses of ecumenical outreach and intercultural discourse, it is fortunate that the developmental process referred to by Langan is an almost inescapable part of the adjustment all religions must make to the powerful forces of contemporary change.

In this new world of intercultural bonds and international communications, there is splendid opportunity to stimulate common effort for the support of human rights. Not only is there an opportunity through theology as a discipline to take an expanded role in fostering intellectual support for these rights as expressed in the United Nations Declaration, but religiously formed persons also have a greatly expanded opportunity to insist upon and campaign for the strengthening of the supportive social processes and institutions which shape cultural mores with respect to rights. Thus, the involvement of religious intellectuals with education means that there can be an urgently needed increase in the emphasis placed upon the moral imperatives underlying human rights. It is clear from these essays that legal systems as such are inadequate to the full task of human-rights vindication. It is clear as well that cultural distortions and deficits prevent the vindication of human rights in many places. Religious leadership for curriculum change, for broad public education, for attacks upon specific obstacles to human-rights exercise are all needed.

Why should learned theologians be engaged in such didactic and popularized concern for the vindication of human rights? The answer is patent—because they, too, are human. There is literally no theology without human beings to relate to a God. Human existence precedes religious formulations. Today it is humanity's existence which is at stake in a world of suicidal nuclear tendencies made infinitely more perilous by the various tyrannies which thrive upon the denial of human rights. It is this compelling reason which must guide the theological community in its concern for this paramount subject.

What can theologians do besides exercise a broader educational role on this subject? They can attempt to influence in a much stronger way than in the past the status groups in their society who hold power. They can do this through mobilizations that focus on war and repression as the two greatest destructive forces pitted against human rights. Renegade groups, whether in or out of power, have at their command terrible weapons and systems for cruelty, and these must be diminished. Further, they can contend with those cultural lags and inequities which compromise human rights due to social prejudice and inertia. Disparities of social structure, acceptance of destructive social institutions—some of them modern engines of economic development—and abusive practices enshrined in cultural patterns must be dealt with bravely. This means mobilization of opinion, campaigns of liberalizing creativity, and pressure from intellectually respected leadership. The development of a humane technology—indeed a technology in service of human rights—is needed. This could be a communications system, for instance, exclusively devoted to tracking the most severe problems of human-rights denial, which today is so extensive that only a computerized data bank of violations can contain a listing of all the terror and misery involved.

Aside from assuming the roles of teacher, advocate, persistent protagonist, leader of opinion, communicator of humane intentions, and arbiter of religious defense of human dignity, theologians must alter social codes and professions, especially law and the military, to insure that societies will agree to sanctions that enforce human-rights protection. These sanctions can take many forms, not just the old, primitive ones of force against violators in the form of military reprisal. The world is now sufficiently complex that there is available a whole range of possible sanctions not previously utilized as social defenses of human rights. Pioneering endeavor in this area of juridical and social activism must be furthered.

If those who study humankind's relation to God are unable to protect God's creatures, then their scholarship is dross. Kenneth Inada, from the Buddhist tradition, indicates the wondrous scope of the calling to recognize and realize and enhance the bonds among all created things and the drive to seek the well-being of others. Because of the splendid amplitude of his vision and the vision of his tradition, his essay came closest to satisfying my desire for a comprehension of the breadth of the challenge that faces us in the field of human rights. How many religions do we know about through the archaeology of their ceremonial sites which have remained after vast destructions that overcame their societies? Is this the way in which our currently living theologies will be memorialized on a planet purged of humanity, on a devastated planet?

9.

HUMAN RIGHTS AND TECHNOLOGY

Hendrik B. Koning

It is my intent to highlight some of the aspects of the interaction among technology, culture, and religion, and, I hope, to make the reader aware of the great need for an ongoing interdisciplinary dialogue with respect to the human development of science and technology.

Changes which are brought about by a science-based technology can have such an overwhelming impact—the introduction of nuclear technology in warfare, for example, with the dropping of atomic bombs over Hiroshima and Nagasaki—that they lead us to the immediate realization that further development of such technology for weaponry should be banned. Those who have control over such weaponry have in their hands the destiny of the lives of hundreds of millions of human beings. This use of nuclear potential for war purposes has had a very negative impact on an objective evaluation of the enormous potential of nuclear energy for peaceful purposes.

In the field of medical technology, until recently, it would have been difficult to envision the necessity for a discussion of what death means. However, the potential for transplanting organs and the introduction of artificial pumps and arteries force us to rethink the question of death from ethical, legal, and theological viewpoints. The tremendous potential of technology to aid those who suffer and the high cost directly related to the prolonging of life raise such questions as: Is everything which is technically possible therefore good? Should techniques such as genetic interference be used at all? What is economically feasible in preventing the death of a person? Should life be prolonged even if it means a person's living as a "vegetable"? Who will decide on policy, and on what basis? Can adherents of various religions ever come to an agreement, or will the consensus be found outside the religious communities? Will it be decided—as seems to be the case with the U.N. human-rights declaration—in a secular way, becoming a statement with which many religious bodies will still have to struggle, on such issues as the role of women?

The development of our telecommunications creates the possibility for a person in possession of a television set to be present at most world events. The use of this medium in what is sometimes referred to as a "global village" is of utmost importance for our understanding of one another. The fact that Americans could see what happened on the front lines in Vietnam made a profound impact; one simply does not easily wipe out the impression made by seeing

Hendrik B. Koning (Episcopalian), a Worker Priest, is a staff engineer in the Philadelphia Electric Company, on assignment to the Philadelphia Urban Coalition. A graduate of the Royal Netherlands Naval Academy, he chairs the Ethics Committee of the Technology and Society Division of the American Society of Mechanical Engineers.

children burned by napalm—another technological invention. One does not easily forget the sight of starving masses.

The appearance of Sputnik and the space travel which followed were technological developments greeted by both fear and enthusiasm about what humanity could achieve. For the first time, a human being could be freed from the gravity which till then had held him or her bound to the earth and its atmosphere. It also raised theological questions about the possibility of human life elsewhere in the universe. The space program made an impact on how we look at ourselves. To see the first pictures of earth from outer space and to see the earth rising over the sun give us an opportunity to reflect with awe about the concept of one world—a finite world in which millions of human beings exist, human beings in a wide variety of cultures and belief systems, whose collective decision-making processes and policies for techno-economic development will greatly affect their lives.

The impact of computer technology is felt throughout society. Much personal information about credit and employment is stored in data banks, and the ethical use of such information is of great concern. The computer has enabled us to extend the capabilities of our brain power with a direct consequence on the lives of many a professional who has become redundant once the knowledge was stored in computer banks. Knowledge accumulated in New York can be used throughout the world via cable or satellite connection, provided one has sufficient financial means and can speak the computer language. Coupling computers with machines makes possible factories without assembly-line workers—again, a development with potential for both good and evil. Who will safeguard its ethical use, and how will the transitions in human lives be handled?

This has been referred to as the age of genocide. The universal tragedies which have taken place in the twentieth century would not have been possible without science and technology. For example, the Holocaust could not have occurred without modern transportation, the use of chemicals, and the construction of gas chambers. The combination of inhuman acts against humanity in many countries raises the question of whether peaceful development and use of the sciences and technology are even possible.

And still we have the secular challenge as formulated in the Universal Declaration of Human Rights. This type of secular challenge is not new in the Western world. We have had to deal with it before. Religious institutions are not always able to lead; at times they become reluctant followers in accepting new realities. When Nicholas Copernicus pointed to a new concept of the solar system, in which the earth was no longer the center, it challenged Christian theology to reformulate the theological pronouncements which used the symbolism of a two-dimensional world. Those Christians who hold to a literal interpretation of the Bible in some respects have a great difficulty in accepting the findings of science and technology, especially when new archaeological technology demands that a biblical interpretation change from a literal to a symbolic one.

Painting the development of our present way of thinking in broad strokes, we notice that, from the seventeenth century on, a religious worldview which included the sciences no longer held together. A scientific, technological world-view developed, with a religious one parallel to it. Increasingly, people came to believe that the human race could determine its own destiny, shape its own institutions, and control social forces. Historians of science and technology have described the complexity of the interaction which took place in the Scientific Revolution in various ways. In essence, it was felt that people who based their thinking of the physical world on the scientific method perceived cause-and-effect relationships. They applied this scientific way of thinking to their social world as well. This secular development questioned the explanations which were once advanced as fate or God's will.

Arend Th. van Leeuwen, in his book *Christianity in World History: The Meeting of the Faiths of East and West*,[1] grappled with this Western development from a Judeo-Christian perspective. He used the word "ontocracy" for a civilization based upon an apprehension of cosmic totality, suggesting that the crucial point of the Bible, both Old and New Testaments, is that the ontocratic view is rejected without compromise in the name of theocracy. Hendrik Kraemer, in the foreword of this work, pointed out: "The only other place, besides Israel, where emancipation from the ontocratic conception of man and world has been realized, is Greece, though here it was on the different basis of the logos in man."[2] Van Leeuwen attempted, said Kraemer, to interpret the peculiarly dynamic character of Western civilization and its worldwide explosive effect, particularly in the present revolutionary stage of technocracy which is creating an unprecedented crisis for all religions, including Christianity.

The application of technology and the resulting technocracy have been seriously questioned over the past 100 years, and they are increasingly questioned today. In the last century, the Amish reacted negatively to technological development, refusing to enter the new industrial era by using electricity and motorized power. They saw the horrors of the early factories, the horrors of what men could do to men in the mines. They saw the horrible conditions for women and children in the factories. They concluded that the industrial lifestyle was contrary to God's will. The Amish religious community still witnesses today to a reaction against uncontrolled change.

Let us also remember the Luddites, who in sheer desperation went out to destroy the machines in the early nineteenth century. At that time the Christian church was identified with the ruling classes, just as it still is today in much of the world. Brave voices were heard in the church, but generally the church spoke only in terms of an agricultural society—which is still the case in many places. The voices of the Luddites can be heard again today, and withdrawal from the world can be seen in the appearance of modern communes, the groups of young

---

[1]Trans. H. H. Hoskins (New York: Charles Scribner's Sons, 1966).
[2]Ibid., p. ix.

people who refuse to be part of the competitive world. In many cases we hear that work has become meaningless, that real life begins after the workday is finished.

We are entering an age of untold possibilities for good as well as evil. Rethinking what it means to have been given dominion over the earth is an awesome challenge. Periods of great change in the past were always periods of great suffering, and it seems that the changes in the near future will be increasingly more rapid and profound. Finding solutions for equitable transitions will not only require an attitude change toward technology; it will also require learning to set policy on an interdisciplinary basis. It is important that the religious community be part of this decision-making process. Scientists and engineers may question why we should bring in religion at this stage. The answer is that, if religion is concerned with the ultimate reality for humankind, then religious beliefs will be reflected in the lifestyle of its adherents. The need for dialogue is great, especially when we interfere with lifestyles.

When we build a railroad through an area where the population lives in the Stone Age, we may create an anthropological disaster. How, then, are we going to deal with the human rights of such a group of people, when we know that millions of people can be fed if the land on which these Stone Age people live is developed? I recall the remarks of an engineer from India who had a leading role in energy development in Northern India. In that country the potential is great for serving the starving masses with energy directed toward food production. As a Hindu engineer, he had to come to terms with utilizing rivers which are regarded as holy. As a Western engineer viewing this problem from a Judeo-Christian viewpoint, I had no difficulty with the conclusion at which he arrived. If necessary, the sacred cows must be set aside when they interfere with the feeding of the hungry masses.

If we read the articles in the Universal Declaration of Human Rights concerning a standard of living adequate for the health and well-being of all people, and if in affirming these rights we commit ourselves to making this a reality, it is hard to imagine how all this can be accomplished without an appropriate development of technology in many countries. Despite all the difficulties which that transition will require, science and technology, appropriately directed, hold out great hope for humanity.

In the scientific and technological communities, there is an increasing awareness of the role of servant to humanity. A symbolic sign of this awareness can be seen in recent changes in the codes of ethics for engineers. Where once the relationship to employer and client took precedence, most codes now state that engineers should uphold and advance the integrity, honor, and dignity of the engineering profession by using their knowledge and skill for the advancement of human welfare.

Interdisciplinary discussion is now a more common practice. The American Association for the Advancement of Science, along with other societies, is actively pursuing the human-rights issue. The voices are still too few, but they are heard. As long as they are, there is hope for more adequate solutions to the problems which face our world.

10.

HUMAN RIGHTS IN THE CONTEMPORARY WORLD: SOME NOTES FROM AN ECONOMIST

Noel J. J. Farley

I approached the reading of the seven theological essays with some trepidation, for the task at hand involved my straying from a straight-and-narrow professional path. I am an economist whose life has been spent in the industrialized West, where Christian values have been present and where the emphasis of the economics I was taught was on how the integration and harmonization of the actions of each leads to the achievement of the interests of each and all. In this mainstream of economics much has been made of enlightened self-interest, but there has been only a limited search for the basis of the perception of this self-interest.[1] There is no assumption that the intent behind individual actions has components of benevolence and malevolence toward others.[2]

From my perspective as an economist, I interpret the focus of these essays as being on policy. The economist has a keen interest in policy, in crossing the bridge from the side of the river which represents the imperfect world to the side which represents the more ideal. The interest of normative economics is in making the move from "what is" to "what should be." Given this central preoccupation, the focus of the essays is on the rights of individuals and on the responsibilities or duties which accompany those rights. This involves the spirit or motivation which underlies one-on-one interactions as well as the two-way interactions between the individual and society.

J. Robert Nelson's essay provides a classification of human rights which encompasses most of the rights mentioned in the essays. He distinguishes between (a) rights to be secured, which he calls political and civil rights, and (b) rights to be provided for and satisfied, which cover economic, cultural, and social rights. A great deal of attention is given to laying a philosophical and/or theological foundation for individual human rights. The dignity of the human being is underlined, and rights and duties consistent with that dignity are identi-

---

[1]As exceptions, I think of the work of Veblen, Duesenberry on the consumption function, and Galbraith.

[2]In the economic literature there is an excellent book which covers a range of issues raised in this essay: K. E. Boulding, *Economics as a Science* (New York: McGraw Hill, 1970), especially chap. 6.

Noel J. J. Farley (Roman Catholic) is Professor of Economics at Bryn Mawr College. He earned his Ph.D. at Yale University and has taught at Boston College, Goucher College, and Swarthmore College. Among his recent articles is "The Functional Distribution of Income in Ireland's Manufacturing Sector, 1956-1973," in the January, 1982, *Economic and Social Review*.

93

fied. Tyrannies which are inconsistent with freedom of choice, religion, speech, and the press are condemned, and—in an economic perspective—the framework is being set for the individual to play a role within the economic and social system.

But, if rights are understood, will duties to others be fulfilled? There are no guarantees of this. Religious thought has its role to play in influencing human action. Believers in Western secularized values also have a role to play. While the economist, as a social scientist, insists that much of his or her endeavor is spent in value-free analyses, the fact cannot be ignored that the economic ethic is one of many influences, for good or ill, which mold the way individuals and societies go about their interactions.

At times there is full consistency between the messages economic and political thought on human rights is trying to convey, and at other times there is not. In part, this is because the economist is subject to diverse religious, cultural, political, and social influences which direct the way he or she proceeds in the science. In particular, religious teaching on social issues is not uniform. For example, some diversity of religious messages is conveyed in the area of the right to life. As a result, some economists provide models of family planning with detailed policy proposals. Other economists, starting with different perspectives, do not accept these proposals and instead emphasize the potential of human productivity in the economic realm and insist on the search for methods of organizing societies which permit the many to have the necessary minimal subsistence rather than for only a few to enjoy material affluence.

There is also a lack of consistency in these messages because different economists, starting out with different weightings of individual human rights, work out the cause-and-effect relationships between initiating action and the total effects on the society. From one kind of economic perspective, there may be a good case for the society to provide resources, for example, to control population growth. This route recognizes that the Malthusian influence may be present, that population control by relying on adjustments of the death rate imposes human suffering, and that some program of population control is the only humane route available to allow the fruits of human ingenuity in the economic realm to grow more quickly than does the expansion of the human race. By this means, rights to be provided for and satisfied can be achieved more easily. In some religious traditions, it is abhorrent to improve the material well-being of a population by casting out the unborn, the infirm, and the unworthy. Undoubtedly, this makes life more difficult for those whose mission it is to concern themselves with rights to be provided for and satisfied.

Economists also disagree because cause-and-effect relationships in their models produce different results. Most often this does not involve a disagreement about values but rather about the conclusions derived from economic analysis. Here, the onus is on the economist to lessen the divergence between the conclusions of the analysis by improving the quality of scientific inquiry.

In the dynamics of human interaction within an economic and social system, there are many competitors in the process of forming values.[3] Some are espousing the same values; others are not. But all of us are under a range of influences. Economists must be aware of this and see part of their mission as informing and being informed by those outside their own profession. The religious teacher must also be aware that prescriptions for human beings in the world can be enriched by social scientific analyses. Such a teacher must be careful that the declared set of human rights are compatible, one with another. At times, it may be that the achievement of one right creates great difficulty for achieving another. It is in this perspective that the economist may be of some help.

In the work on comparative economic systems, the economist has used a variety of success criteria.[4] In some of these models, consumer sovereignty is mentioned as a success criterion with much emphasis laid on individualism and freedom of choice. Alternatively, some models lay out planners' preferences as a priority with an emphasis on the societal interest as perceived by a central authority. Efficiency is laid out as another success criterion. This concept has particular meaning to the economist, as it involves the achievement of a "first best" economic world at any moment of time. Also mentioned is the achievement of economic growth, which is presumed to be consistent with the individual and the societal interest. Finally, there is often reference to equity in the distribution of income and wealth. Here there is often lack of definition. Analyses often simply refer to less and more equal distributions of income, wealth, and economic opportunity.

Having set out these success criteria, the economist does not systematically justify them or give them varying weights of importance in the scheme of priorities. Generally, conventional values lead to the acceptance of either consumer or planner preferences. Efficiency studies, which are of importance to the economist, take on meaning only when preferences are specified. The growth goal takes on a life of its own in many studies. For some economists—for example, D. Seers[5] and H. B. Chenery[6]—economic development takes on meaning only within a distributional framework, and there is no guarantee that modern economic growth will produce equity in the distribution of income. But the economist, as a social scientist, has little to say about what an equitable distribution of income is. In the history of economic analysis, there was a time when a scientific basis was laid for the appropriateness of an equal distribution of income, but that time has passed, and it is now understood that no such case has been made. At present, the economist has regard for ethical considerations,

[3]See ibid., chap. 6.
[4]E.g., see B. Balassa, *The Hungarian Experience in Economic Planning* (New Haven: Yale University Press, 1959), pp. 5-24.
[5]D. Seers, "The Meaning of Development," *International Development Review*, vol. 11, no. 4 (December, 1969), pp. 2-6.
[6]H. Chenery et al., *Redistribution with Growth* (London: Oxford University Press, 1974).

thereby giving recognition to the noneconomic sources of what is considered to be just and equitable.

All this underlines that, whether or not the economist wishes it, economic work has some influence on the formation of values. The same is true of religious teaching, but both groups live in a world which is pluralistic in terms of influences, and each must appreciate the character of its role and the limitation on its influence in value-formation.

All that having been said, it must be recognized that the economist has a realm of her or his own. That realm creates a focus on the study of scarcity and exchangeable goods. Within this perspective, the economist examines the effects of human interaction at the societal level. There is an "opportunity cost"[7] to action, and there are trade-offs to be executed. There are also necessary trade-offs among societal goals. At times, for example, historical evidence suggests that to have consumer sovereignty is to lay aside the possibility of maximizing the rate of economic growth. There can be similar trade-offs (or conflicts) between achieving planner sovereignty and efficiency, efficiency and equity, and equity and consumer sovereignty. Often, analysis suggests that different economic systems perform well by different criteria. Examples abound of these kinds of conclusions in works on economic policy.

Reading the human rights and duties laid out in the seven essays, an economist is struck by the conflicts which can exist between these rights in the framework of an economic system. To me, these trade-offs are not recognized in these essays. This blind spot leads to a lack of reflection on how to specify the outlines of an economic system which could contribute to economic betterment. The religious thinker assumes that the question either is outside the domain of his or her competence or is unimportant in the sense that, if the individual decision-maker is well informed by her or his faith's social teaching, the fate of the human condition will take care of itself. In this perspective, systems matter only insofar as it is understood that they give recognition to the importance of human rights; beyond that, everything depends on the qualities of mind and heart which underlie individual decisions.

Probably this is as it should be. The focus of the religious thinker is inevitably on the nature, character, and human potentiality of the individual and the two-way relationship between God and creation. Yet, religious thinkers do influence the way humans can go through their economic lives. Sometimes, the social message creates difficulty for the human condition. Returning to the right to life as an example, the position taken by many religious thinkers has enormous ramifications for the economic prospect. Such an example cries out for a commitment among scientists, philosophers, and theologians to understand one another and to reach together, in a cooperative division of labor, for models of

---

[7]I.e., the cost of doing something in terms of one's loss of opportunity to do something else with the same resources (time, money, etc.).

thought which more coherently spell out the dimensions of a desirable economic system. The economist needs religious thought to inform his or her value judgments more systematically. Religious thought in the social and economic context needs the insight that social scientific results can provide on the degrees of complementarity and substitutability among the range of individual human rights.

A reading of these essays seems to bring out problems with the content of economic rights in the industrialized countries. Economic rights refer particularly to minimum economic security. The poor and the disadvantaged are to be cared for by the fortunate. But, in societies where the guarantee of minimum economic security can be achieved easily and where labor is highly productive in the economic realm, what is to be done with the remaining fruits of labor after this minimum guarantee is met? Is there to be a commitment to equality in the distribution of income within these societies? To what degree should there be redistributions of income from the industrialized to the less-developed countries? These value questions are hardly posed in these essays, but, it should be added, they have been raised elsewhere in other religious writings.

This is a strange lack of emphasis, given the focus on the Universal Declaration of Human Rights. It is an unfortunate deemphasis also, because the North-South conflict of recent years has been sparked by income inequalities in the world and the belief of the less-developed economies that their economic conditions are linked to the actions of the Western industrialized nations. The way in which the international dimension to human rights generally, and to economic rights especially, works itself out may speak loudly in the long run to the manner in which human dignity is viewed and handled in both the industrialized and the less-developed countries of the world.

Overall, however, these essays are timely. We have lived through a period when there has been much reference to political- and civil-rights violations. Economic difficulties have also abounded with the experience of stagflation in the industrialized countries and both famine and dim prospects for economic betterment in many less-developed countries. It is appropriate, then, to focus again on human rights and examine how these rights can be assured. There is much work yet to be done.

11.

PSYCHIATRIC ISSUES ON HUMAN RIGHTS IN RELIGION

Perry Ottenberg

The opportunity to critique these seven religious perspectives on human rights presents a challenge. The pluralism of religious viewpoints shown in these essays undermines any single concept of what is right. A pluralism in psychiatry also provides a rheostat for comparisons of different patients' behavior, or that of the same individual, depending on capabilities, experience, and health. Most people are so self-centered that they have only a poorly conceived sense of social responsibility. Often, through the journey of personal discovery provided in psychotherapy, the patient becomes more flexible in thinking about religious attitudes. Occasionally, anxious and rebellious patients can grow to accept responsibility for religious practices in the commonweal.

The practice of clinical psychiatry which I shall use to discuss these essays is rooted in the medical viewpoint that all human behavior, including religious behavior, has an overdetermined meaning. Everything human has a tenuous hold on rationality. Each person's childhood, genes, and society are the basic reservoir for an explanation of his or her current behavior. By and large, human behavior is the result of huge unconscious forces in people's minds. A psychiatrist focuses on current human frailty within any social context and often takes a reduction-ist stand to avoid the type of questions raised by these articles. Psychiatry focuses on what is and how it came about, not on what ought to be. It sees all human behavior as a calculus of choices rather than as being judged from absolute ideas of good or evil, right or wrong, pure or impure. At times, one's super-ego, or conscience, acts in an absolute fashion, but this, too, is part of understanding each person's background from the childhood phase of development.

Does each author confront him or herself with appropriate questions about the human-rights reality of a given religion? Does each author take some stand that is not merely defensive about that religion's invidious practices? Many discriminatory customs are accepted in routines of seating, reading scripture, admission to holy places, recognition in religious politics, representation in religious schools, and access to ordination. Most religious groups are excessively traditional: religious roles contain the stereotypes of ancient history in an unchallenged form in a rapidly changing world.

These essays are a step toward scrutiny of sensitive human-rights issues. However, there is a paucity of discussion about racism, homosexuality in the

---

Perry Ottenberg (Jewish) is Senior Attending Psychiatrist at the Institute of Pennsylvania Hospital in Philadelphia. He is a graduate of Harvard College and Harvard Medical School, where he worked with Talcott Parsons. He chairs the Committee on Emerging Issues of the American Psychiatric Association and is the author of numerous articles.

congregation or among the clergy, women's rights, abuse of authority, misuse of orthodoxy, and the limits of fundamentalism. There were no comments on sickness, narcissism, and human failure in religious leadership; no comments on the pathology of religious bureaucracy, with its devastating impact on ordinary people; no discussion on the transmission of irrational hatred among religious groups through the generations; little discussion of how established religions help to reinforce economically and racially discriminatory attitudes in their society.

From a psychiatrist's viewpoint, it is the individual and the family who form the core meaning of human rights. Each man, woman, or child is a unique universe more significant than the state or religion. Clinical psychiatry can assist in correcting persistent attitudes and practices which are institutionalized in society and religion and which seriously restrict the personal fulfillment of most of the world's population. The United States and other Western societies—because of their history of multiple religions, separation of powers, economic wealth, and social mobility—allow for more individual expression than do homogeneous or totalitarian states.

A psychiatrist assists individuals to recognize their uniqueness as persons separate from and interdependent with the family, state, and religion. Common values have been internalized into their thinking and behavior. It is easy to talk with a person's public personality, but it often takes years of careful psychotherapy to reach the private, innermost personality. It is rare for religious leaders, as it is rare for other leaders, to recognize their own institutionalized biases. A psychiatrist is also prone to unchallenged, internalized social biases. If two psychiatrists belong to the same professional school of thought, they are unlikely to challenge in each other an acceptable social exclusiveness about "others."

The capacity to challenge one's own religious practices becomes essential to a discussion of comparative human rights from different religious viewpoints. Psychiatry is one of the first therapeutic fields in medicine to recognize the caricatures of social roles which people have internalized from a lifetime of living unexamined lives in dominating social structures. Most humans crave certainty through religion in the face of life's overwhelming burdens. Since one finds in religious beliefs only the chimera of transcendent existence outside the human body, the existential burden of random life and death is unresolved.

Religious bureaucracies tend toward conservatism and cozy arrangements with their governments. Hand-in-glove cooperation between leaders of state and religion contributes to the individual's helplessness when confronted by institutionalized resistance to social change. It is not a "sickness" to oppose the state or religious institutions of one's society. To carry a protest sign across Red Square, to fast for political ends in South Africa or Ireland, to eat matzoh, to demand an abortion, to sue for divorce, to sing songs, or to create art and theater is a human celebration of courage.

Excessive faith and religious conformity might be a psychiatric problem. Healthy prayer differs from obsessive rituals. Realistic views of death differ from suicidal preoccupations. For many believers the strength of peer-group attitudes may take over the critical role of painful self-examination needed to avoid sheep-like conformity.

Women's rights in religious belief systems require women's equal status and treatment with men. An inferior status has been accorded women through the ages in most of the world's religions, as is especially apparent in regulations concerning abortion, birth control, divorce, child custody, and equal inheritance rights. Educational and political exclusion follows the pattern of ecclesiastical exclusion.

Economic rights in religion are reflected in how different church bureaucracies distribute their patronage and select their leaders. Indentured working conditions are widespread. If people are economically desperate, illiterate, intimidated by the state, and exhorted by their own religious leaders to submit, they have a right to resist and fight for change.

Health rights in religion include concerns for prenatal care, nutrition of mother and child, access to medically safe abortion, sex education, prevention of treatable diseases, proper stimulation and education for children, and care for the handicapped and those who fail to strive. Protection of the rights of those who cannot protect themselves is both a governmental and a religious duty. The incarcerated, sick, aged, handicapped, infirm, and especially the intellectually deficient are the wards of society.

Ecological rights in religion are now challenging various religious leaders. The explosive spread of technology has impinged on our global health and future resources. Nuclear dangers, toxic wastes, greenhouse effects in the atmosphere, fossil fuel by-products, and carcinogens arouse legitimate fears of our survival as a species. Human rights are slowly being extended to include the protection of the total global environment; this understanding underlies recent religious positions about a nuclear freeze.

Religious rights include the freedom to worship according one's own conscience, to disobey under specified conditions, and to preserve inviolable places of worship from invasion and desecration. Civil disobedience is a matter of conscience, as is conscientious objection.

Individual rights which impinge on religious values include the rights of adult gays and lesbians to a private life. Unpopular psychosocial views, while they make us uncomfortable, are a painful reality which must be protected in every religion, or there is no freedom for anyone. A strong religion is one in which the adherents allow alternate viewpoints. A cohesive sense of unity emerges out of affiliation, not out of unchallenged conformity.

The Universal Declaration of Human Rights is a tidal swell to protect all of us—including women, children, prisoners, the mentally ill, the handicapped, minorities, and religious groups—from our own protectors. From a psychiatric viewpoint, every human being needs assistance to achieve full potential. Problems of private identity, family conflict, class differences, and international rivalry are ubiquitous. Women should be treated as a private individuals and not as the brood mares of society. Children, often in large families, need freedom to become independent from their role as social insurance policies for their parents. Homosexuality is still so threatening to political and religious leaders that it arouses enormous resistance in traditional and fundamentalist religions.

The past 150 years have seen a rapid breakdown in the stabilizing influence of set expectations in life provided by the family, small community, homogeneous value system, and religious conformity. Wars, migration, technology, instantaneous communication, public education, and prolonged human survival reflect the continuing churning of our world's cultures, classes, and religions.

Human-rights awareness is a reflection of one's biopsychosocial maturity. Each person has an internalized image of self which includes an ability to evaluate the normative belief systems in his or her society. Each individual now tests the social world and belief systems which heretofore were simply accepted. Just as the world is now a traveler's toy, so the varieties of religious experiences are part of shopping around for an identity. Social mobility is also part of comparative religious mobility. Anyone could fit into another society, religion, or sex role depending on the accident of birth. Trans-religious mobility is not yet as widespread as intermarriage and social migration will allow it to be in the future.

Psychiatry holds to a view of the individual's right to a feisty struggle to cross cultural, class, religious, and political lines. While the family, community, and religion are bases for emotional security, they can also be shackles of conformity, conservatism, and compromise supporting outmoded historical myths and values. Human life with an identity is the long-term unfolding of malleable protoplasm into different biopsychosocial cultures and religions. Life with a personality takes years to develop and is *sui generis*. Everyone should have the opportunity to get through the toll booths of social institutions into a broad expanse of growth and creativity.

Sexual taboos, with their associated guilt, are still so threatening to most people that we are decades away from accepting the rights of adolescents to their own patterns of sexual mores. The technological impact of the pill and other contraceptives, the automobile, ease of travel, media stimulation, lessened parental supervision, rapid social migrations, and the use of alcohol and other drugs reinforces increasing opportunities for adolescents for greater sexual activity. Church and society currently maintain restrictive views of sexuality, abortion, and family planning, which sacrifice individual human rights and capitulate to doctrinaire attitudes. The individual is subordinated to the collective belief-systems of religion. The Talmud, Qur'an, Gita, and Old and New Testaments are idealized statements which are not necessarily rooted in current social reality. Documents are not people. Constitutions do not generally reflect the way a society operates in social reality.

The Universal Declaration of Human Rights is a revolutionary document on a wave of social change. Human-rights issues will rock entire societies and religions which do not adapt to technology, media influences, cross-cultural contacts, and individual rights. Universal human rights exclude the accidents of birth—sex, color, ethnicity, class, and religion—from invidious predetermined roles in life. Constant revision and respect for individual and societal differences are needed to avoid sacrificing each new generation's children to institutional imprisonment.

Psychiatry can assist in the pursuit of human rights by demonstrating how myopic one can be in opposing, pursuing, or moderating any human-rights issue. One can be sick whether one is for, against, or neutral about any human-rights activity. Being for social change does not protect one from illness. Jim Jones, a modern messiah, led his mostly poor, black followers to death in the jungles of Guyana. Many children who were placed with him through the state of California's foster care program died for his narcissistic glory. Narcissistic expansion is an occupational hazard for those in eminent positions of power.

Human rights in Protestantism. Protestantism put the individual's rights above the Catholic Church in Luther's time. In Freud's time, psychiatry liberated the individual from the strictures of society. Both entities are now part of the establishment in Western society, but many Protestant churches and psychiatric groups have been co-opted by their societies. Collective governmental domination that serves a power elite is spreading all over the globe. Various forms of autocracy and totalitarianism are inimical to both Protestantism and psychiatry, wherever they occur. From a psychiatric viewpoint, it would be helpful in the common cause for the Protestant churches to challenge restrictive governmental and church policies which deprive citizens of equal protection under the law.

Human rights in Eastern Orthodoxy. The traditional Eastern Orthodox Church emphasized one's duty over one's rights, traditional observances over social change, sinfulness over creativity, and discipline over freedom of choice. Psychiatry requires each patient to evaluate in depth her or his existing relationships in family, marriage, or church, challenging many conservative expectations. Reification of thought or religious practices ends up as dogma or ritual. From a psychiatric perspective, concretized thinking restricts social change. Intolerant social structures in the Middle East and in the lands now comprising the Soviet Union have crippled human rights for centuries under the auspices of religion. Major obstacles to peace in Cyprus, Israel, Lebanon, or Ireland require supranationalistic and suprareligious cooperation. Psychiatry has a major contribution to make in understanding irrational behavior, conflict resolution, ethnocentric perceptions, prejudice, discrimination, terrorism, hostage behavior, "brainwashing" techniques, and care for victims and their families. Religion and psychiatry are mutually related human-care institutions which ought to work together.

Human rights in Roman Catholicism. In many areas of the world, the Catholic Church has had a long history of cooperation with civil authorities who held power and wealth. Support for psychiatry, health care, education, women's rights, the sharing of power, and political mobility hardly existed. With recent social encyclicals, worker priests, ecological awareness, and the reduction of membership, the Catholic Church is in transition. Liberation for women to control decisions about their bodies has met with traditional Catholic Church obstacles. The Equal Rights Amendment has been seen in distorted terms. Human rights in the deepest sense challenge bureaucracy, traditionalism, and the state. Because church institutions are resistant to change, many people view religion as an obstacle, when it is instead the personnel who misinterpret the precepts and teachings who should be confronted.

Human rights in Judaism. Human rights in Judaism are mingled with the problems of the Jewish State in Israel, terrorism, and the rights of the Palestinians. The history of the Nazi extermination of 6,000,000 Jews, including 1,500,000 children; expulsion from England, France, and Spain; and centuries of inquisition and pogroms—all are part of the history of the diaspora. Sensitivity to the individual in Judaism is linked to fierce self-preservation in the face of overwhelming odds. Psychiatry has studied the origins, dynamics, and forms of dehumanization which contribute to genocide. None of the essays nor the Declaration of Human Rights considers this efficient, technological elimination of humans in any detail. Dehumanization is a modern form of the violation of human rights which cannot be developed adequately here. It relieves otherwise-sensitive humans from overwhelming guilt, compassion, identification, and empathy with their fellows. Bypassing human restraints through dehumanization is a common disease of the industrial world, going beyond the dynamics of prejudice. Prejudice requires hate, fear, and involvement. Dehumanization is quiet, bureaucratic, and total.

Human rights in Islam. Traditionalism holds sway over most of the Muslim world. Ideal Islamic theory and Muslim practice have to be reconciled. Apostasy from traditional Islam is punishable by death, a practice not supported by the Qur'an. Women are equal to men, yet they are not allowed to interpret the Qur'an. They have experienced centuries of institutionalized inferiority, and they have little access to divorce, abortion, sex education, mobility, political power, child custody, or occupational opportunities. There is an increasing danger to human rights from fundamentalist and fanatical Islamic dictatorships. Their impact on women, children, and minorities challenges the existence of human rights on a day-to-day level.

Human rights in Buddhism. From a psychiatric view, Buddhism places little emphasis on the individual, self, or social activism. A 2,500-year history reinforces the acceptance of a rigid social structure. Self-contemplation after extraordinary training can lead to a feeling of transcendence and cosmic union, which can avoid human-rights issues. The desire in Buddhism to extinguish realistic human rage, urges, and other basic drives runs counter to psychiatry's attempt to recognize and channel these drives into increased self-awareness and pro-social action. Buddhism can be seen as emphasizing ritualistic withdrawal from social reality to the self. This state of contemplation is similar to many altered states of consciousness, all of which share massive passivity and diminished concern for the complexity of human-rights issues.

Human rights in Hinduism. Caste status is a brand of inequality and discrimination. It is ascribed, not achieved. Caste, in a psychiatrist's opinion, represents a massive ego-blow to the emergent personality. Being held in an inferior state in life is not the problem, but rather that less intelligent, less sensitive, less deserving individuals take away one's just deserts through their arbitrary use of power. Caste reflects millenia of institutionalized and religiously supported discrimination. Hinduism as a religious tradition emphasizes duties rather than individuals' rights. A psychosocial viewpoint would consider that caste values infringe on one's human rights from birth, leading to modifications in one's self-awareness, aspirations, and attitudes toward authority. Racism in South Africa or the United States has broad similarities to caste issues, as it also judges people outside an achievement viewpoint.

Those of us who are involved in this exchange of views about human rights come from different cultures, language groups, nations, and religious backgrounds. Most of us are members of groups which have in the past been treated as chattel, drafted into wars of unknown purpose, hounded, killed, or vilified for our values by other, dominant groups. Human rights are no mystery to the objects of dehumanization, exploitation, and discrimination in political, economic, health, religious, and sexual matters. It does not take a Ph.D. to recognize a sign which reads, "Keep out!" "Go to the rear!" "Sit upstairs!" "Members only!" "Unwelcome!" "Conform or get out!"

Psychiatry views the anthropological diversity of human societies, styles of behavior, family life, sexuality, and religious practices as evidence that no single religion has a corner on the truth market. There exists such diversity of family styles, sexual activity, and ritual belief-systems that Western psychiatry has focused on the individual's adjustment to his or her social group and self. This individual focus of psychiatry makes institutional needs secondary to the person's needs. Psychiatry's task is to put the isolated, powerless, weak person ahead of his or her state or religion. It seeks to ameliorate the collective reality, which is supported by apathy, denial, and exploitation, and which leads to pandemic illness and shared social pathology. From a psychiatric viewpoint, the immense power of the state or of organized religion does not give either one the right to restrict the full growth or choice of any woman or child or nonconformist.

UNIVERSAL DECLARATION OF HUMAN RIGHTS
(Approved by the United Nations General Assembly on December 10, 1948)

Preamble

Whereas recognition of the inherent dignity and of the equal and inalienable rights of all members of the human family is the foundation of freedom, justice and peace in the world,

Whereas disregard and contempt for human rights have resulted in barbarous acts which have outraged the conscience of mankind, and the advent of a world in which human beings shall enjoy freedom of speech and belief and freedom from fear and want has been proclaimed as the highest aspiration of the common people,

Whereas it is essential, if man is not to be compelled to have recourse, as a last resort, to rebellion against tyranny and oppression, that human rights should be protected by the rule of law,

Whereas it is essential to promote the development of friendly relations between nations,

Whereas the peoples of the United Nations have in the Charter reaffirmed their faith in fundamental human rights, in the dignity and worth of the human person and in the equal rights of men and women and have determined to promote social progress and better standards of life in larger freedom,

Whereas Member States have pledged themselves to achieve, in co-operation with the United Nations, the promotion of universal respect for and observance of human rights and fundamental freedoms,

Whereas a common understanding of these rights and freedoms is of the greatest importance for the full realization of this pledge,

Now, therefore,

The General Assembly

Proclaims this Universal Declaration of Human Rights as a common standard of achievement for all peoples and all nations, to the end that every individual and every organ of society, keeping this Declaration constantly in mind, shall strive by teaching and education to promote respect for these rights and freedoms and by progressive measures, national and international, to secure their universal and effective recognition and observance, both among the peoples of Member States themselves and among the peoples of territories under their jurisdiction.

Article 1

All human beings are born free and equal in dignity and rights. They are endowed with reason and conscience and should act towards one another in a spirit of brotherhood.

Article 2

Everyone is entitled to all the rights and freedoms set forth in this Declaration, without distinction of any kind, such as race, colour, sex, language, religion, political or other opinion, national or social origin, property, birth or other status.

Furthermore, no distinction shall be made on the basis of the political, jurisdictional or international status of the country or territory to which a person belongs, whether it be independent, trust, non-self-governing or under any other limitation of sovereignty.

Article 3

Everyone has the right to life, liberty and the security of person.

Article 4

No one shall be held in slavery or servitude; slavery and the slave trade shall be prohibited in all their forms.

Article 5

No one shall be subjected to torture or to cruel, inhuman or degrading treatment or punishment.

Article 6

Everyone has the right to recognition everywhere as a person before the law.

Article 7

All are equal before the law and are entitled without any discrimination to equal protection of the law. All are entitled to equal protection against any discrimination in violation of this Declaration and against any incitement to such discrimination.

Article 8

Everyone has the right to an effective remedy by the competent national tribunals for acts violating the fundamental rights granted him by the constitution or by law.

Article 9

No one shall be subjected to arbitrary arrest, detention or exile.

Article 10

Everyone is entitled in full equality to a fair and public hearing by an independent and impartial tribunal, in the determination of his rights and obligations and of any criminal charge against him.

Article 11

1. Everyone charged with a penal offense has the right to be presumed innocent until proven guilty according to law in a public trial at which he has had all the guarantees necessary for his defence.
2. No one shall be held guilty of any penal offence on account of any act or omission which did not constitute a penal offence, under national or international law, at the time when it was committed. Nor shall a heavier penalty be imposed than the one that was applicable at the time the penal offence was committed.

Article 12

No one shall be subjected to arbitrary interference with his privacy, family, home or correspondence, nor to attacks upon his honour and reputation. Everyone has the right to the protection of the law against such interference or attacks.

Article 13

1. Everyone has the right to freedom of movement and residence within the borders of each State.
2. Everyone has the right to leave any country, including his own, and to return to his country.

Article 14

1. Everyone has the right to seek and to enjoy in other countries asylum from persecution.
2. This right may not be invoked in the case of prosecution genuinely arising from nonpolitical crimes or from acts contrary to the purposes and principles of the United Nations.

Article 15

1. Everyone has the right to a nationality.
2. No one shall be arbitrarily deprived of his nationality nor denied the right to change his nationality.

Article 16

1. Men and women of full age, without any limitation due to race, nationality or religion, have the right to marry and to found a family. They are entitled to equal rights as to marriage, during marriage and at its dissolution.
2. Marriage shall be entered into only with the free and full consent of the intending spouses.
3. The family is the natural and fundamental group unit of society and is entitled to protection by society and the State.

Article 17

1. Everyone has the right to own property alone as well as in association with others.
2. No one shall be arbitrarily deprived of his property.

Article 18

Everyone has the right to freedom of thought, conscience and religion; this right includes freedom to change his religion or belief, and freedom, either alone or in community with others and in public or private, to manifest his religion or belief in teaching, practice, worship and observance.

Article 19

Everyone has the right to freedom of opinion and expression; this right includes freedom to hold opinions without interference and to seek, receive and impart information and ideas through any media and regardless of frontiers.

Article 20

1. Everyone has the right to freedom of peaceful assembly and association.
2. No one may be compelled to belong to an association.

Article 21

1. Everyone has the right to take part in the government of his country, directly or through freely chosen representatives.
2. Everyone has the right of equal access to public service in his country.
3. The will of the people shall be the basis of the authority of government; this will shall be expressed in periodic and genuine elections which shall be by universal and equal suffrage and shall be held by secret vote or by equivalent free voting procedures.

Article 22

Everyone, as a member of society, has the right to social security and is entitled to realization, through national effort and international co-operation and in accordance with the organization and resources of each state, of the economic, social and cultural rights indispensable for his dignity and the free development of his personality.

Article 23

1. Everyone has the right to work, to free choice of employment, to just and favourable conditions of work and to protection against unemployment.
2. Everyone, without any discrimination, has the right to equal pay for equal work.
3. Everyone who works has the right to just and favourable remuneration ensuring for himself and his family an existence worthy of human dignity, and supplemented, if necessary, by other means of social protection.
4. Everyone has the right to form and to join trade unions for the protection of his interests.

Article 24

Everyone has the right to rest and leisure, including reasonable limitation of working hours and periodic holidays with pay.

Article 25

1. Everyone has the right to a standard of living adequate for the health and well-being of himself and of his family, including food, clothing, housing and medical care and necessary social services, and the right to security in the event of unemployment, sickness, disability, widowhood, old age or other lack of livelihood in circumstances beyond his control.
2. Motherhood and childhood are entitled to special care and assistance. All children, whether born in or out of wedlock, shall enjoy the same social protection.

Article 26

1. Everyone has the right to education. Education shall be free, at least in the elementary and fundamental stages. Elementary education shall be compulsory. Technical and professional education shall be made generally available and higher education shall be equally accessible to all on the basis of merit.
2. Education shall be directed to the full development of the human personality and to the strengthening of respect for human rights and fundamental freedoms. It shall promote understanding, tolerance and friendship among all nations, racial or religious groups, and shall further the activities of the United Nations for the maintenance of peace.
3. Parents have a prior right to choose the kind of education that shall be given to their children.

Article 27

1. Everyone has the right freely to participate in the cultural life of the community, to enjoy the arts and to share in scientific advancement and its benefits.
2. Everyone has the right to the protection of the moral and material interests resulting from any scientific, literary or artistic production of which he is the author.

Article 28

Everyone is entitled to a social and international order in which the rights and freedoms set forth in this Declaration can be fully realized.

Article 29

1. Everyone has duties to the community in which alone the free and full development of his personality is possible.

2. In the exercise of his rights and freedoms, everyone shall be subject only to such limitations as are determined by law solely for the purpose of securing due recognition and respect for the rights and freedoms of others and of meeting the just requirements of morality, public order and the general welfare in a democratic society.

3. These rights and freedoms may in no case be exercised contrary to the purposes and principles of the United Nations.

Article 30

Nothing in this Declaration may be interpreted as implying for any State, group or person any right to engage in any activity or to perform any act aimed at the destruction of any of the rights and freedoms set forth herein.

SELECTED BIBLIOGRAPHY

Protestant

Asheim, Ivar, ed. *Christ and Humanity*. Philadelphia: Fortress Press, 1970. (For the Lutheran World Federation.)
Brownlie, Ian, ed. *Basic Documents on Human Rights*. Oxford: Clarendon Press, 1971.
Commission of the Churches on International Affairs. *Human Rights and Christian Responsibility*. Report of the Consultation, St. Pölten, Austria, 21-26 October 1974. Geneva: World Council of Churches, 1975.
Cunningham, A.; Miller, D.; and Will, J. "Toward an Ecumenical Theology for Human Rights." New York: Commission on Faith and Order, National Council of Churches, 1980 (photocopied).
The Ecumenical Review, vol. 27, no. 2 (April, 1975). Especially articles by David Jenkins, Alice Wimer, Burgess Carr, and Gustav Wingren.
Falconer, Alan D., ed. *Understanding Human Rights*. Dublin: Irish School of Ecumenics, 1980. Especially chapters by José Miguez-Bonino, Martti Lindqvist, Jürgen Moltmann, and Alan Falconer.
Forell, George W., and Lazareth, William. *Human Rights: Rhetoric or Reality*. Philadelphia: Fortress Press, 1978.
International Review of Mission, vol. 66, no. 263 (July, 1977). Especially articles by José Miguez-Bonino and John Perkins.
Lissner, J., ed. *Theological Perspectives on Human Rights*. Geneva: Lutheran World Federation, 1977.
Lissner, J., and Sovik, A. *A Lutheran Reader on Human Rights*. Geneva: Lutheran World Federation, 1978.
Miller, Allen O., ed. *A Christian Declaration of Human Rights*. Grand Rapids, MI: W. B. Eerdmans, 1977. (For the World Alliance of Reformed Churches.)
Paton, David, ed. *Breaking Barriers, Nairobi 1975*. Grand Rapids, MI: W. B. Eerdmans, 1976.

Orthodox

Harakas, Stanley. *Contemporary Moral Issues Facing the Orthodox Christian*. Minneapolis: Light and Life Publishing Co., 1982.
---. *Let Mercy Abound: Social Concern in the Orthodox Church*. Brookline, MA: Holy Cross Orthodox Press, 1982.
---. "Orthodox Social Conscience," in Demetrios J. Constantelos, ed., *Orthodox Theology and Diakonia: Trends and Prospects*. Brookline, MA: Hellenic College Press, 1981, pp. 187-208.
---. *Toward Transfigured Life: The Theoria of Orthodox Christian Ethics*. Minneapolis: Light and Life Publishing Co., forthcoming.
Tsirintanes, Alexandros. *Towards a Christian Civilization*. Athens: Damascus Publications, 1950.

Roman Catholic

Calvez, Jean-Yves, and Perrin, Jacques. *The Church and Social Justice: The Social Teaching of the Popes from Leo XIII to Pius XII*. Chicago: Henry Regnery, 1961.
Ehler, Sidney, and Morrall, John, eds. *Church and State through the Centuries: A Collection of Historic Documents*. London: Burns and Oates, 1954.
Finnis, John. *Natural Law and Natural Rights*. New York: Oxford University Press, 1980.
Gremillion, Joseph, ed. *The Gospel of Peace and Justice: Catholic Social Teaching since Pope John*. Maryknoll, NY: Orbis, 1976.
Hennelly, Alfred, and Langan, John, eds. *Human Rights in the Americas: The Struggle for Consensus*. Washington, DC: Georgetown University Press, 1982.

Hollenbach, David. *Claims in Conflict: Retrieving and Renewing the Catholic Human Rights Tradition.* New York: Paulist, 1979.
Maritain, Jacques. *The Rights of Man and the Natural Law.* New York: Scribner's, 1945.

Jewish

Belkin, Samuel. *In His Image.* New York: Abelard-Schuman, 1960.
Fisher, Eugene, and Polish, Daniel, eds. *Formation of Social Policy in the Catholic and Jewish Traditions.* Notre Dame, IN: University of Notre Dame Press, 1980.
Hirsch, Richard. *There Shall Be No Poor.* New York: Union of American Hebrew Congregations, 1965.
Kellner, Menachem Marc, ed. *Contemporary Jewish Ethics.* New York: Sanhedrin Press, 1978.
Konvitz, Milton R., ed. *Judaism and Human Rights.* New York: W. W. Norton & Co., 1972.
Vorspan, Albert, and Lipman, Eugene. *Justice and Judaism.* New York: Union of American Hebrew Congregations, 1956.

Muslim

Ali, P. S. *Human Rights in Islam.* Lahore: Aziz Publishers, 1980.
Beg, A. "Civil and Political Rights in Islam," *Al-Ittihad* (Muslim Students Association, Indianapolis), vol. 14, no. 1-2 (January-April, 1977), pp. 41-48.
Brohi, A. K. "Islam and Human Rights," in A. Gauhar, ed., *The Challenge of Islam.* London: The Islamic Council of Europe, 1980, pp. 176-195.
Hakim, K. A. *Fundamental Human Rights.* Lahore: Institute of Islamic Culture, 1975.
Jullundhri, R. A. "Human Rights in Islam," in Falconer, *Understanding Human Rights* (above), pp. 34-46.
Maududi, A. A. *Human Rights in Islam.* Lahore: Islamic Publications, 1977.
Nadvi, S. M. *Human Rights and Obligations* (in the light of the Qur'an and Hadith). Lahore: Shaikh Muhammad Ashraf, 1974.
Parwez, G. A. "Bunyadi Haquq-e-Insaniyat (Fundamental Human Rights)" (Urdu), *Tulu'-e-Islam* (Lahore), November, 1981, pp. 18-40.
Patel, R. *Women and Law in Pakistan.* Karachi: Faiza Publishers, 1979.
Qutb, M. *Islam: The Misunderstood Religion.* Lahore: Islamic Publications, 1972.

Buddhist

Bhandarkar, D. R. *Asoka.* 3rd ed. Calcutta: University of Calcutta, 1955. (Discusses King Asoka, the man, his place in history, and his famous rock and pillar edicts.)
Dayal, Har. *The Bodhisattva Doctrine in Buddhist Sanskrit Literature.* London: Kegan Paul, Trubner, Trench & Co., 1932. (One of the earliest studies on the doctrine.)
de Silva, Padmasiri. *Value Orientations and Nation Building.* Colombo, Sri Lanka: Lake House Investments, Ltd., 1976. (A monograph that brings classical Buddhist thought to the contemporary scene on human needs, causes of struggle, and war and peace.)
Khantipalo, Phra. *Tolerance: A Study from Buddhist Sources.* London: Rider & Co., 1964. (A meticulous, penetrating study on the subject.)
Malalasekera, G. P., and Jayatilleke, K. N. *Buddhism and the Race Question.* Paris: UNESCO, 1958. (Helpful monograph by two outstanding Theravāda thinkers.)
Rahula, Walpola. *What the Buddha Taught.* 2nd enlg. ed. New York: Grove Press, 1974. (One of the best on basic doctrines; appendix includes two relevant texts—*Advice to Sigāla [Sigālovāda-sutta]* and *The Words of Truth [Dhammapada]*.)
Swearer, Donald K., ed. *Secrets of the Lotus: Studies in Buddhist Meditation.* New York: Macmillan Co., 1971. (A good source for understanding the various types of meditation—classical and contemporary.)

113

Hindu

Bühler, Georg. *The Laws of Manu*. New York: Dover, 1969.
Derrett, J. Duncan M. *Introduction to Modern Hindu Law*. Bombay: Oxford University Press, 1963.
Gandhi, M. *None High, None Low*. Editor and publisher, A. T. Hingorani. Bombay: Bharatiya Vidya Bhavan, 1961.
Ghosal, U. N. "The Relation of Dharma Concept to the Social and Political Order of the Brahmanical Canonical Thought," *The Journal of Bihar Research Society* 38 (March, 1952): 190-202.
Masani, R. P. "Caste and the Structure of Society," in G. T. Garratt, ed., *The Legacy of India*. Oxford: Clarendon Press, 1937.
Radhakrishnan, S. P. *The Hindu View of Life*. London: Allen and Unwin, 1961.
Tagore, R. *Religion of Man*. Boston: Beacon Press, 1961.
Varma, V. P. "Studies in Hindu Political Thought and Its Metaphysical Foundation," *The Journal of Bihar Research Society* 38 (March, 1952): 35-116.
Zaehner, R. C. *Hinduism*. London and New York: Oxford University Press, 1962.

Social-Historical

Arendt, Hannah. *The Origins of Totalitarianism*. New York: Harcourt, Brace, 1951.
Hobbs, Albert. *Man Is Moral Choice*. New Rochelle, NY: Arlington House, 1979.
McCloy, Shelby T. *The Humanitarian Movement in Eighteenth-Century France*. Lexington: University of Kentucky Press, 1957.
Marcel, Gabriel. *Man against Mass Society*. Chicago: Henry Regnery, 1962.
Watkins, Frederick. *The Political Tradition of the West: A Study in the Development of Modern Liberalism*. Cambridge, MA: Harvard University Press, 1940.
Weintraub, Karl Joachim. *The Value of the Individual*. Chicago: The University of Chicago Press, 1982.

Technological

Albrecht, Paul, ed. *Faith and Science in an Unjust World*. 2 vol. Philadelphia: Fortress Press, 1980. (Plenary presentations and reports and recommendations from an ecumenical discussion of science and faith and science and society in a world perspective.)
Barbour, Ian G. *Science and Secularity*. New York: Harper and Row, 1970. (On the ethics of technology and the relationship between religion and science.)
Conference on Engineering Ethics. New York: American Society of Civil Engineers, 1975. (Conference co-sponsored by eight engineering societies in Baltimore, May, 1975.)
Ladriere, Jean. *The Challenge Presented to Cultures by Science and Technology*. Paris: UNESCO, 1977. (Author is philosopher and scientist.)
Modern Technology: Problem or Opportunity? Daedalus, vol. 109, no. 1 (Winter, 1980). (Collection of essays raising questions for future discussion.)
van Leeuwen, Arend Th. *Christianity in World History: The Meeting of the Faiths of East and West*. London: Edinburgh House Press, 1965. (Of interest to engineer and scientist from a religious perspective.)

Economic

Friedman, Milton and Rose. *Free to Choose: A Personal Statement*. New York: Harcourt Brace Jovanovich, 1980.
Galbraith, John Kenneth. *The Affluent Society*. Boston: Houghton Mifflin, 1959.
Heilbroner, Robert. *An Inquiry into the Human Prospect: Updated and Reconsidered for the 1980s*. New York: Norton, 1980.
Ward, Barbara. *The Rich Nations and the Poor Nations*. New York: Norton, 1962.

Wallich, Henry. *The Cost of Freedom: A New Look at Capitalism.* New York: Harper and Brothers, 1960.

Psychiatric

Bernard, Viola; Marmor, Judd; and Ottenberg, Perry. "Psychodynamics of Group Opposition to Health Programs." *American Journal of Orthopsychiatry* 30 (April, 1960): 330-345.

Bernard, Viola; Redl, Fritz; and Ottenberg, Perry. "Dehumanization." Chapter 8 of *Sanctions for Evil*, ed. Nevitt Sanford. San Francisco: Jossey-Bass, Inc., 1971.

Ottenberg, Perry (chairperson of Committee on Social Issues). "Emotional Aspects of School Desegregation." *Committee Report #37B*. New York: Group for the Advancement of Psychiatry, September, 1970.

—————. "Violence in the Family: Abused Wives and Children." *Bulletin of American Academy of Psychiatry and Law* 5 (1977): 380-389.

—————. "The Physician and Social Issues." Chapter 6 of *Psychiatry in General Medical Practice*, ed. Gene Usdin and Jerry M. Lewis. New York: McGraw Hill, 1979.

—————. "Terrorism." *Psychiatric Annals* 10 (May, 1980): 179-185.